Contemporary English

Second Edition

Book 2

Jeanne Becijos & Jan Forstrom

McGraw Hill **Contemporary**

Acknowledgements

I dedicate my work to my patient and understanding husband, Tom Keating—Jan Forstrom

The authors and publisher would like to thank the following people for their help and contribution to the second edition of *Contemporary English:*

First Edition authors: Claudia Rucinski-Hatch, Cheryl Kirchner, Elizabeth Minicz, Mechelle Perrott, Kathryn Powell, Cecelia Ryan, Ardith Loustalet Simons, Kathleen Santopietro Weddel

Series Consultant: **Catherine Porter,** Adult Learning Resource Center, Des Plaines, IL
Grammar Consultant: **Sally Gearhardt,** Santa Rosa Jr. College, Santa Rosa, CA

Reviewers: **Jack Bailey,** Program Coordinator, ESL and Foreign Language, Santa Barbara City College, Santa Barbara, CA; **Kenneth Bretz,** ESL Teacher, Cupertino-Sunnyvale, Cupertino, CA; **Kristine Colina,** Instructor, Crystal Lake Community School. Broward County, FL; **Dianne Gibson Birdsall,** Instructor, College of DuPage, Glen Ellyn, IL; **Ionela Istrate,** Sr. Director, Adult Ed and ESOL, YMCA of Greater Boston, Boston, MA ; **Barbara Kremer,** ESOL Director, New Americans Center, Lynn, MA ; **Liz Minicz,** Department of Adult Education co-chair, William Rainey Harper College, Palatine, IL; **Paula Orias,** Site Administrator, Piper Community School, Broward County, FL; **Mary Pierce,** Director, Xavier Adult Education Center, New York, NY; **Kathryn Powell,** Instructor, William Rainey Harper College, Palatine, IL **Annette Ruff-Barker,** Instructor, College of DuPage, Glen Ellyn, IL; **Kristin Sherman,** Instructor, Central Piedmont Community College, Charlotte, NC; **Shirley Taylor,** Project SCALES, West Newton, MA ; **Deborah Thompson,** Instructor, Los Angeles Unified School District, Los Angeles, CA; **Yindra Vanis,** Instructor, Morton College, Cicero, IL

Special thanks to Mike Eagan and Kathy Feilen for their contributions to Reading for Real, page 29.

Photo Credits

Page 5: Spencer Grant/PhotoEdit; Page 12: Spencer Grant/PhotoEdit
Page 17: Getty Images/Zigy Kaluzny; Page 24: Paul Conklin/PhotoEdit
Page 29: Mary Kage Denny/PhotoEdit; Page 36: Rhoda Sidney/PhotoEdit
Page 41: Thinkstock; Page 48: A. Ramey/PhotoEdit, Rudi Von Briel/PhotoEdit, John Neubauer/PhotoEdit
Page 53: Getty Images/Bruce Ayres; Page 60: Ian Oddie/PhotoEdit
Page 65: Bill Aron/PhotoEdit, Bill Aron/PhotoEdit; Page 72: David Young-Wolff/PhotoEdit
Page 77: © Corbis; Page 84: Robert Brenner/PhotoEdit, Michael Keller/Index Stock
Page 89: Robin Sachs/PhotoEdit; Page 96: © Jose L. Pelaez/Corbis or © Jose L. Pelaez/The Stock Market, Larry Lawver/Index Stock
Page 101: Billy E. Barnes/PhotoEdit; Page 108: Dana White/PhotoEdit
Page 113: Robert Brenner/PhotoEdit; Page 120: Robert Brenner/PhotoEdit

Executive Editor: Linda Kwil
Senior Editor: Paula Eacott
Art Director: Michael E. Kelly
Production Manager: Genevieve Kelley
Interior Design: William Seabright and Associates
Interior Illustration: Andrew Lange, Don Petersen, David Sullivan
Cover Illustration: Don Petersen

McGraw Hill | **Contemporary**

Contents

About This Series

Program Components and Philosophy

Contemporary English is a four-level, interactive, topic-based ESL series for adult learners ranging from the high-beginning to the low-advanced level. The series includes

- **Student Books** for classroom use,
- **Workbooks** for independent use at home, in the classroom, or in a lab,
- **Audiocassettes** or **CDs** for individual student, classroom, or lab use,
- **Teacher's Annotated Editions,** with reproducible activity masters and unit progress checks for assessment, and
- **Conversation Cards,** for extra oral pair practice of unit vocabulary and grammar.

These materials have been correlated to the following Federal and state standards: the SCANS (Secretary's Commission on Achieving Necessary Skills) Competencies, CASAS Competencies, California Model Standards, the BEST standards, and the Florida LCPs.

Contemporary English empowers students to take charge of their learning and to develop strong communications skills for the real world. Each unit falls under one of the following broad topics: Home and Neighborhood, Family Relations, Employment and Opportunity. In short, the series addresses topics of interest and concern to adult learners.

Unit Structure of the Student Books

Contemporary English provides a controlled and predictable sequence of instruction and activities. Conveniently for teachers, each page of a unit functions as a self-contained mini-lesson. Each unit is divided into two parts, each of which begins with a **Scene** that presents incidents from the lives of newcomers to the United States or aspects of U.S. culture that students encounter regularly. A series of discussion questions proceeds from factual comprehension of the **Scene** to personalization and, in Books 3 and 4, to problem solving.

After each **Scene** comes **Vocabulary** presentation through art or controlled definitions. In Books 3 and 4, students are encouraged to use dictionaries to discover word meanings. Each vocabulary section ends with an exercise that checks basic comprehension of the target words.

Following the vocabulary exercise is a focused listening task that includes pre-listening and post-listening work. **Listening** presents target content and language structures through lively conversations and other samples of natural speech, such as telephone answering-machine messages and transportation announcements.

Throughout Contemporary English, grammar structures are first contextualized in the **Scenes** and listening activities and then presented, practiced, and applied on follow-up **Spotlight** pages. Appearing three times in each unit, the **Spotlight** pages model target structures in contexts related to the unit topic. Special **Spotlight** boxes present the target structures schematically and provide brief, straightforward explanations when necessary. Exercises following the structure presentations allow students to manipulate the structures in meaningful contexts.

Following controlled structure practice on the **Spotlight** pages, listening and speaking skills are developed further in the **Pair Work** activities. Recorded two-person conversations explore the unit topics, structures and vocabulary in natural, colloquial language. Students listen to a conversation and practice it. Students then use this conversation as a model and work in pairs to create their own dialogue. **Spotlight** pages end with a **Your Turn, Talk About It,** and / or **In Your Experience** activity providing communicative application of the new structures.

These last three features occur within the units at specific points, after students have been exposed to structures or ideas in more controlled exercises. **Your Turn** is an oral follow-up to reading, listening, or structure practice. Students can complete the activity alone or in pairs. **Talk About It** is an oral group activity, allowing students to interact within larger groups, applying the vocabulary and structures they have just learned in a personalized conversation. **In**

Your Experience, a writing activity that draws on students' prior knowledge and experiences, allows learners to relate the topics to their own lives.

Contemporary English helps students develop their reading skills and become motivated readers of English through **Reading for Real. Reading for Real** includes such real-life documents as a winning job résumé, instructions for office voice mail, biographies of real people, advice from the local police, and ads for cellular phone plans. Follow-up **Talk About It** activities extend and personalize the reading.

In Books 1 and 2, **Organizing Your Ideas** introduces the concept of visual literacy through the use of graphic organizers. T-charts, Venn diagrams, and idea maps help students generate their own ideas on questions related to unit topics. The oral activity at the end of the page encourages students to share and compare their ideas with their classmates.

In Books 3 and 4, **Organizing Your Ideas** is replaced with **Understanding Charts (Tables, Maps, Graphs),** which focuses on information graphics. These activities help students learn to read, interpret, and use information in a graphic format—skills that are crucial in the workplace and in GED preparation. The page concludes with a follow-up activity in which learners develop their own simple graphs or charts and share them with the class.

Problem-solving and critical-thinking skills are developed further in **Issues and Answers,** which contains short letters with views of U.S. life from a variety of perspectives, including those of immigrants and their "cultural advisors." The follow-up activity on this page asks students to use the ideas they generated on the previous page to help the letter-writer solve his or her problem.

Community Involvement provides a channel for students to discover useful inside information about life in the United States. From using the post office to contacting the city council, **Community Involvement** encourages students to go out and explore their neighborhoods. Alternative activities are available for those students who are unable to do research outside of class. No matter which activities are chosen, the information students find will help them adapt to a culture that can be difficult to understand. In-class follow-up activities help students integrate cultural knowledge with their language skills.

At the very end of each unit is **Wrap-Up,** a project requiring students to use a graphic organizer such as a T-chart, a Venn diagram, an idea map, or a timeline to brainstorm, organize ideas, and then use their ideas to present project to the class. Following **Wrap-Up** is the self-assessment activity **Think About Learning,** a final reflection that asks students to evaluate the quality of their own learning on the major content points, life skills, and language structures in the unit.

Contemporary English is centered around the needs of adult ESOL students: to communicate effectively in English at home, at work, and in their communities. It provides opportunities for adult ESOL students to learn both the language and the culture of the United States.

Icons

Contemporary English uses the following icons throughout the series:

Listening: All Scenes, Listening activities, and Pair Work dialogues are recorded on tape and CD.

Grammar: These exercises may require a variety of language skills, but the main focus is practice of the structure found in the Spotlight box.

Critical Thinking: These exercises require students to perform an activity that requires some analysis or evaluation of information.

Scope and Sequence Book 2

Unit Name/ Number	Vocabulary	Grammar	Language Functions	Graphic Literacy
1 **People and School** *Pages 2–13*	• Adult Education • Schedules • Application	• **Review:** Present of Be • **Review:** Past of Be • **Review:** Can and Can't • **Recycle:** Negative present of Be with contractions • **Recycle:** Past of Be in yes/no questions, short answers, and prepositions of time	• Ask and answer questions about grades and ages • Share information about your family and friends • Talk about your education and class schedule	• Read information from a class schedule • Make a future class schedule
2 **Relax!** *Pages 14–25*	• Outings • Exercise • Recreation Classes	• **Review:** Simple present • **Recycle:** Prepositions of place • **Present:** Possessives • **Present:** Reflexive pronouns	• Talk about various leisure activities • Discuss recreational classes offered in your area • Talk about things you enjoy doing	• Use a Venn diagram to compare types of recreation and their costs • Complete a chart to explain what you like and dislike
3 **Problems in the Neighborhood** *Pages 26–37*	• Crime • Local Government • Safety	• **Review:** There is, there are • **Review:** Simple past • **Review:** Simple past with irregular verbs • **Recycle:** Simple present in information questions • **Present:** There was, there were	• Talk about your neighborhood • Compare new and old neighborhoods • Voice your concerns about your neighborhood	• Use a chart to explain what you like and dislike about your neighborhood
4 **Timecards and Paychecks** *Pages 38–49*	• Shifts • Pay • Deductions • Overtime	• **Review:** Information questions in the past • **Recycle:** Can in yes/no questions and short answers • **Present:** Past time words • **Present:** Past Progressive	• Ask and answer questions about work schedules • Discuss benefits at work • Explain a mistake on a paycheck	• Use a day planner to prioritize tasks
5 **Shape up!** *Pages 50–61*	• Health Problems • Supplements • Rest	• **Review:** Subject and object pronouns • **Recycle:** Simple present in yes/no questions and short answers • **Present:** Future with be + going to • **Present:** Count and non count nouns	• Role-play a conversation about exercise • Talk about things you do for exercise • Discuss healthy living	• Use an idea map to explain reasons and ways to exercise • Complete a survey about the exercise habits of others
6 **Bargain Hunting** *Pages 62–73*	• Deals • Price • Quantity • Resale	• **Recycle:** Like to, want to, need to + verb • **Present:** Comparative adjectives • **Present:** Superlative adjectives • **Present:** Too + adjectives and quantifiers	• Share ideas about bargain hunting • Debate which item is a better buy • Talk about the pros and cons of using a credit card	• Use a T-chart to decide how to make future purchases • Make a T-chart to compare the best places to shop
7 **Home Sweet Home** *Pages 74–85*	• Renting • Purchasing a Home • Living Expenses	• **Review:** Present progressive • **Recycle:** Simple present • **Present:** Future with will • **Present:** Future progressive	• Discuss the details of a rental application • Describe the responsibilities of owning a house • Compare renting vs. buying a home	• Use a T-chart to compare expenses for renting and buying a home
8 **Using the Library** *Pages 86–97*	• Library Procedures • Library Resources • Book categories	• **Recycle:** Can in yes/no questions and short answers • **Present:** Demonstrative adjectives • **Present:** Could and would for requests • **Present:** Direct and indirect objects	• Ask and answer library card application questions • Talk about library resources • Practice questions to ask a librarian	• Use a table to categorize various books by genre
9 **You're Hired** *Pages 98–109*	• Job Interview • Resume • Job Types • Forms	• **Review:** Verb + infinitive • **Recycle:** Affirmative simple past • **Present:** Must, must not, have to, don't have to • **Present:** Compound sentences with and....too, and....either	• Tell about your past job experience and qualifications • Suggest ways to prepare for an interview • Give advice about conduct at work	• Understand job skills and job options using an idea map
10 **Getting Around: Public and Private Transportation** *Pages 110–121*	• Fares • Transportation Schedules • Travel	• **Recycle:** Have to and had to • **Present:** Should and ought to • **Present:** May and might • **Present:** Can and be able to	• Role play a conversation about how to travel downtown • Describe the differences between public transportation in different countries • Tell the class about the different ways that you travel around town	• Use a table to describe public transportation in your city, and its advantages and disadvantages

Problem-Solving	Community Involvement	EFF	SCANS	CASAS
• Resolve a scheduling problem for an adult who needs to find time to study	• Collect information about adult schools in your community	• Learn new skills • Educate self and others	• Foundation skills • Knowing how to learn	**P. 5**, 7.2.7, **P. 7**, 7.1.1, **P. 8**, 7.4.9 **P. 9-10**, 7.1.2, **P. 12**, 2.5.5
• Plan recreation on a budget • Discuss the problems of employment when it interferes with leisure time	• Discover and report community recreation information through the use of various media	• Provide for physical needs • Provide for emotional needs	• Foundation skills • Sociability	**P. 16**, 0.2.4, **P. 17**, 2.6.1, **P. 19**, 0.2.1, **P. 22**, 7.2.3, **P. 24**, 7.4.3
• Discuss problems with and suggest solutions for neighborhood crime • Investigate a new neighborhood before relocating to avoid possible problems	• Learn about your city government • Write a letter to a city council member about a problem in your neighborhood	• Identify and monitor problems, community needs, strengths, and resources • Influence decision-makers and hold them accountable	• Foundation skills • Problem solving	**P. 29-30**, 5.6.1, **P. 31**, 7.2.3, **P. 34**, 7.2.6, P. 35, 7.3.2, **P. 36**, 5.1.6
• Calculate an employee's gross pay and net pay	• Survey friends and classmates to find how various companies pay employees	• Manage work process and resources	• Foundation skills • Understands how systems work • Organizes and maintains information	**P. 39**, 6.1.5, **P. 41**, 1.8.2, **P. 42**, 4.8.6, **P. 46**, 4.7.4
• Offer advice about weight loss • Plan an exercise schedule with a partner	• Research free health screening services in your community	• Pursue personal self-improvement	• Foundation skills • Responsibility	**P. 51**, 2.5.3, **P. 53**, 3.4.5, **P. 55**, 7.4.8, **P. 56**, 3.5.9, **P. 58**, 6.6.5
• Compare cost of purchasing an item with cash to using a credit card	• Find coupons from different businesses in your community	• Help self and others	• Foundation skills • Self-management • Decision-making	**P. 63**, 1.3.1, **P. 64**, 1.2.2, **P. 65**, 1.2.1, **P. 66**, 1.3.3, **P. 67**, 1.3.2, **P. 72**, 1.3.5
• Assist a worried wife about deciding to rent or buy a home	• Locate housing assistance information in your community	• Put ideas and directions into action	• Foundation skills • Acquires and evaluates information	**P. 76**, 1.4.2, **P. 77**, 1.4.1, **P. 78**, 1.4.6, **P. 79**, 7.2.7, **P. 84**, 1.4.6, 7.4.4
• Offer advice to someone who wants to practice English at the library	• Find the library that is closest to your home • Search the internet get information about your local library	• Find and use community resources and services	• Foundation skills • Use materials and facilities wisely	**P. 87**, 2.5.6, 0.2.2, **P. 89**, 2.5.5, **P. 92**, 0.2.1, b, 0.1.2
• Create a list of skills and volunteer work for someone with no job experience	• Find information about job openings in your community	• Meet new work challenges Plan and renew career goals	• Foundation skills • Works within a system • Uses personnel wisely	**P. 99**, 4.1.8, **P. 100**, 4.4.3, **P. 102**, 4.4.1, **P. 103**, 4.1.2, **P. 105**, 4.1.5, **P. 107**, 4.1.7
• Advise someone to share expenses for the use of one car • Create a list of car expenses	• Research and report on different types of transportation where you live	• Find out how systems work	• Foundation skills • Seeing things in the mind's eye	**P. 111**, 2.1.7, P. 113, 2.2.4, **P. 115 & 117**, 2.2.3, **P. 119**, 1.9.6

💡 📼 Scene 1: Conversation

With a partner, talk about the pictures. Listen to the conversation. Ask and answer the questions.

Mario and Tam are on the city bus.

Questions

Where are the two men? Where are they going?
Which man says he's too old for school, Tam or Mario?

What age do you think is too old for school?
Do your friends and family work and go to school? Who?

Vocabulary

Look at the words and pictures. Listen to your teacher. Say the words.

to enroll = to fill out papers to begin a class
too (old, expensive, small . . .) = (older, more expensive, smaller) than something should be

> In some states, 6th grade is elementary school and 9th grade is junior high.

Schools in the United States

preschool
Ages: 2–4 years old

elementary school

Grades	Ages
kindergarten	5 years old
1st grade	6 years old
2nd grade	7 years old
3rd grade	8 years old
4th grade	9 years old
5th grade	10 years old

middle school/junior high school

Grades	Ages
6th grade	11 years old
7th grade	12 years old
8th grade	13 years old

senior high school

Grades	Ages
9th grade	14 years old
10th grade	15 years old
11th grade	16 years old
12th grade	17 years old

adult school

vocational school

university or **college**

Your Words

_____

_____

Exercise 1 Read about Mario's and Tam's families. Complete the sentences. Write the correct word on the line. Use the words above to help you.

1. Mario's niece is two years old. She's in _____preschool_____ .
2. Mario's nephew is seven years old. He's in _____ .
3. Tam's granddaughter is eleven years old. She's in _____ .
4. Mario's sister is 18 years old. Last year, she was in _____ .
5. After high school, Mario enrolled in _____ to learn his job.
6. Tam and his wife enrolled in English class at the _____ .

Listening

Exercise 2 Listen to Mario's friends talking about a family member or a roommate in school. Write the correct school, grade, and age in the chart.

Name	Student	School	Grade	Age
1. Chela	son	elementary	1st	6
2. Mohammed	wife	_____	_____	_____
3. Lin	daughter	_____	_____	_____
4. Francisco	roommate	_____	_____	_____

After You Listen Check your answers with a partner.

Your Turn

With a partner, ask and answer questions about the grades and ages of students. For example, ask "How old are students in vocational school?" "They are 18 to 100+ years old."

SPOTLIGHT on Review Present of Be

Affirmative Statements	Negative Statements	Negative Contractions
I **am (I'm)** a student.	I **am not** a student.	**I'm not** a student.
You **are (You're)** a teacher.	You **are not** a teacher.	**You're not/You aren't** a teacher.
He **is (He's)** in school.	He **is not** in school.	**He's not/He isn't** in school.
She **is (She's)** in school.	She **is not** in school.	**She's not/She isn't** in school.
It **is (It's)** good.	It **is not** good.	**It's not/It isn't** good.
We **are (We're)** students.	We **are not** students.	**We're not/We aren't** students.
They **are (They're)** students.	They **are not** students.	**They're not/They aren't** students.

Questions	Short Answers
Are you a student?	Yes, I **am.**
Is she in school?	No, she**'s not.**

Exercise 3 Read about Tam and his family. Complete the sentences. Write the correct form of <u>be</u> on the line.

My name **(1)** _____is_____ Tam. My wife and I **(2)** _____ from Vietnam. We **(3)** _____ students at City Center Adult School. We **(4) not** _____ in the computer class. We **(5)** _____ in the ESL class. Our son works full-time. He **(6) not** _____ a student. Our grandson **(7)** _____ 20 years old. He **(8)** _____ in vocational school. He wants to be an auto mechanic.

Exercise 4 In your notebook, write about your family and friends. Use the sentences in Exercise 3 to help you. For example, write "My name is _____. I am from _____."

Pair Work

Listen to the conversation between Tam and Mario. Then practice it with a partner.

Tam: Do you have a sister?
Mario: Yes. My sister, Dolores, is 19 years old.
Tam: Is she a student?
Mario: Yes, she is. She's in adult school.

Your Turn

Look at the conversation again. With a partner, make a new conversation. Use information about your friends and family. Use the present tense of **be.** Share your conversation with the class.

Reading for Real

Mario is an assembler at Evanston Electronics. He is reading a sign at work.

Free Computer Classes for Assemblers

Classes start next week,

on Tuesdays and Thursdays after work.

4:00 p.m. to 6:00 p.m.

Employees need to pass a computer test to get a raise.

See your supervisor to sign up for the class.

Exercise 5 Mario wants to take a computer class. Read the questions below. Look for the answers in the sign above. Circle the letter of the best answer.

1. Who can go to classes at Evanston Electronics?
   a. assemblers
   b. supervisors and assemblers
   c. supervisors only

2. What kind of classes are they?
   a. assembly classes
   b. computer classes
   c. English classes

3. How much do the classes cost?
   a. $4.00
   b. $6.00
   c. nothing

4. When are the classes?
   a. every day after work
   b. Tuesday and Thursday
   c. next week only

5. Why is it good to pass the test?
   a. You need to pass to be a supervisor.
   b. You need to pass to be an assembler.
   c. You need to pass to get more money.

6. Who do employees need to see to sign up for classes?
   a. their teacher
   b. their supervisor
   c. their friend

Talk About It

In a group, ask and answer these questions. Can you use a computer? Do you know about any computer classes in your neighborhood? Where are they?

With a partner, talk about the pictures. Listen to the conversation. Ask and answer the questions.

Mario is at City Center Adult School.

> Can I get an application and class schedule for my sister, please? She wants to enroll in some classes.

> Was she a student here last year?

> No, she wasn't. She was in high school last year.

> Hmm. Some of these classes can help me get a raise at work. Maybe I can take a class here.

> One more application, please!

Questions

Why is Mario at the City Center Adult School?

What does Mario's sister want to do? Was Mario's sister a student at City Center Adult School last year?

Why do you think Mario asks for one more application?

Were you in school last year?

Can adult school classes help you at work? How?

Vocabulary

Look at the words and pictures. Listen to your teacher. Say the words.

application

schedule

open

closed

$$$
fee

registration

to take a class = to be a student in a class

Exercise 6 Tell Mario what he needs to do. Circle the letter of the phrase that best completes each sentence.

1. You fill out an application to
   a. take a class or get a job.
   b. ride a bus.
   c. buy a computer.

2. You read a class schedule to find
   a. directions to the school.
   b. the answers for a test.
   c. the times and places for classes.

3. You go to the registration office to
   a. see the doctor.
   b. sign up for a class.
   c. get a driver's license.

4. You cannot take a class if it is
   a. open.
   b. closed.
   c. elementary.

5. You have to pay a
   a. schedule.
   b. registration fee.
   c. application.

Listening

Exercise 7 Mario's sister, Dolores, is signing up to take classes at City Center Adult School. Listen to the information. Write the correct word on the line.

After You Listen Compare your answers with a partner.

Talk About It

In a group, ask and answer these questions. What classes from Exercise 7 do you want to take? Is there a registration fee for any of the classes? What days do the classes meet?

City Center Adult School

Gonzalez		Cristina
Last name	First name	Middle name

Orange Avenue		
Address	Street	Apt.

Riverford		
City	State	Zip code

Telephone number	Social Security number

List the classes you want to take:

Class	Day	Time	Fee
Business Math			

SPOTLIGHT on Review Past of Be

Affirmative Statements	Negative Statements
I **was** a student.	I **was not (wasn't)** a student.
You **were** a teacher.	You **were not (weren't)** a teacher.
He **was** in school.	He **was not (wasn't)** in school.
She **was** in school.	She **was not (wasn't)** in school.
It **was** a good school.	It **was not (wasn't)** a good school.
We **were** students.	We **were not (weren't)** students.
They **were** in school.	They **were not (weren't)** in school.

Questions	Short Answers
Were you a student?	Yes, **I was.**
Was she in the fifth grade?	No, **she wasn't.**

Exercise 8 Mario and Dolores wrote about their educations on their adult school applications. Complete the sentences. Use <u>was</u>, <u>were</u>, <u>wasn't</u> or <u>weren't</u> to make a story about Mario and Dolores.

Mario Gonzalez		Dolores Gonzalez	
School	**Years**	**School**	**Years**
Brown Elementary	1989–1995	Brown Elementary	1990–1996
Townsend Middle School	1995–1997	Townsend Middle School	1996–1998
Palo Verde High School	1997–2001	Palo Verde High School	1998–2002
Benson Vocational School	2001–2002		

1. In 1992, Mario and Dolores _____*were*_____ students at Brown Elementary.

   They **(not)** _____ in high school.

2. In 1996, Mario and Dolores _____ at Townsend Middle School.

3. Mario _____ a student at Palo Verde high school in 1997.

4. In 1997, Dolores **(not)** _____ in high school. She

   _____ in middle school.

5. Mario _____ a student at Benson Vocational School in 2001.

   It _____ a good school. He learned a lot there.

Exercise 9 In your notebook, write sentences about your education or the education of someone you know. Use <u>was</u> or <u>were</u>. For example, write "I was a student in elementary school from 1975 to 1981. My friend Thuy was in first grade in 1972."

Talk About It

In a group, talk about your education or the education of someone you know. Use the sentences from Exercise 9 to help you. For example, say "I was in high school from 1997 to 2001. Math was difficult for me." "My son was a student at the Benson Vocational School last year. It was a good school."

SPOTLIGHT on Review Can and Can't

Affirmative Statements	Negative Statements	Meanings
I **can** understand the lesson.	I **can't** understand the lesson.	Use **can** to talk about **abilities** you have now.
You **can** study at night.	You **can't** study at night.	
He **can** use the computer.	He **can't** use the computer.	

We **can** walk to school.	We **can't** walk to school.	Use **can** to talk about permission or ability in the future.
You **can** buy the book.	You **can't** buy the book.	
They **can** go to class.	They **can't** go to class.	

Questions	Short Answers	
Can I have a schedule?	Yes, you **can**.	Use **can** to make a request.
Can he start school next year?	No, he **can't**. He's too young.	

Remember: **Can't** is the contraction for **cannot**.

Exercise 10 Mario is asking about a computer class. Complete the sentences. Write the correct word on the line. Use <u>can</u> or <u>can't</u>.

Mario: **(1)** _____Can_____ I sign up for the Tuesday/Thursday Computer class?

Office Worker: I'm sorry, you **(2) not** _____. That class is closed. But the Monday/Wednesday class is still open.

Mario: I **(3) not** _____ come to school in the afternoon. I am working. I **(4)** _____ only come in the evening.

Office Worker: Well, you **(5)** _____ take a class on Saturday.

Exercise 11 In your notebook, write sentences about you using <u>can</u> and <u>can't</u>. For example, write, "I can fix a car. I can use a computer. I can't speak Spanish."

Pair Work

Listen to the conversation between the office worker and Mario. Then practice it with a partner.

Office Worker: Can I help you?

Mario: Yes, I want to take a class. Can I take the advanced computer class on Thursday evening?

Office Worker: Yes, you can. The class is still open.

Mario: Great. Can I sign up now, please?

Your Turn

With a partner, make a new conversation. Use information about your schedule and classes. Use **can** and **can't**. For example, say, "I can't take a computer class on Wednesday. I can take the computer class on Thursday." Share your conversation with the class.

Organizing Your Ideas

Dolores has a busy schedule. Are you busy, too? When are you in school? When are you at work? When do you work around the house, do your homework, or help in the community? Fill in this chart with your usual schedule. Write your activities for each morning, afternoon, and evening. When do you usually have free time? Write your free time in the schedule too.

My Schedule

	Sunday	Monday	Tuesday	Wednesday	Thursday	Friday	Saturday
Morning (9:00–12:00)							
Afternoon (1:00–5:00)							
Evening (6:00–9:00)							

Now think of the schedule you want to have in the future. Write the days and times for work below. Write in the names of the classes and when you want to take them. Remember to plan some free time to rest and relax!

My Future Schedule

	Sunday	Monday	Tuesday	Wednesday	Thursday	Friday	Saturday
Morning							
Afternoon							
Evening							

Talk About It

In a group, look at the schedules you have now. How are your schedules different? How are they the same? Talk about the schedules you want to have in the future. What things in your present schedules do you want to change? What do you need to do to make the changes happen?

Issues and Answers

Mario wrote to Abdul for ideas about what to do to learn computers. Read the letter and Abdul's advice. Then talk with other students about the advice. Do you agree? What other advice can you give?

a d v i c e

suggestion; helpful idea one person gives to another

Ask Abdul and Anita

DEAR ABDUL,

My supervisor at work says I can get a raise when I pass a computer test. I can take a free class after work at my company on Tuesdays and Thursdays, but I'm too tired to think after I work for eight hours. How can I learn the computer when I work all day?

—MARIO

DEAR MARIO,

It's important to know how to use the computer at work. You need to find a time to take a computer class. You're lucky. You can take a free class at work. Adult schools also have computer classes at night and on the weekends. Look at your schedule and choose a class.

—ABDUL

Your Turn

Mario needs to find a time he can take a computer class.

Step 1: Make a schedule for Mario's week. Follow the examples of schedules on page 10. Mario works Monday through Friday from 7:00 A.M. to 4:00 P.M. He plays soccer with his friends every Sunday from 1:00 to 3:00 P.M. On Wednesday evenings he takes care of his younger brothers and sisters while his mother goes to Citizenship class from 7:00 to 8:00.

Step 2: Make a list of all the times Mario can take computer classes. Look at the information about the computer class at his job on page 5. Is this a good time for Mario to take a class? Write other times that are good for Mario on your list. Decide which time is the best for Mario to take a computer class. Write in the class on Mario's schedule.

Step 3: Share the schedule you made for Mario with the class. Did another person choose the same time for Mario?

Community Involvement

There are many places adults can go to school. Some elementary schools, middle schools, and high schools have English classes for adults. Adult schools and community colleges have many classes, such as English, electronics, auto mechanics, or citizenship classes. Some classes are free, and others have fees.

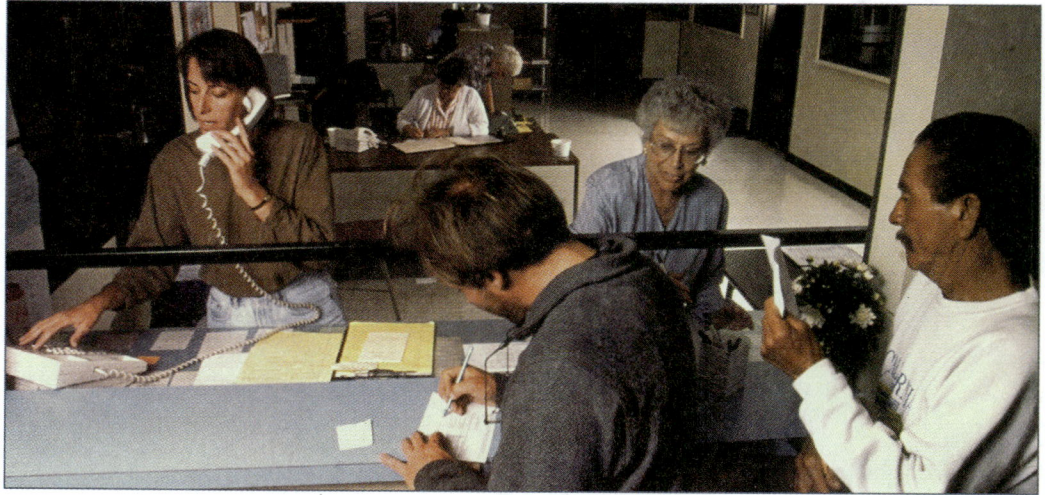

Your Turn

With a partner, talk about classes for adults in your native country and in the United States. What classes do you know about? Where are the classes? Are there fees for the classes?

Community Action

Step 1: Work with a partner. Find information about classes that can help you as a worker, parent, or community member. Use the telephone book, the Internet, information at a library, or ask someone for information. Find the answers to these questions.

· What are the names of other schools for adults in your community? _____
· Where are the schools? _____
· What transportation can you use to go to these schools? _____
· Are there fees for the classes? _____
· When are the classes? _____

Step 2: With your partner, go to the registration office at your school or at another adult school. Get a class schedule. Choose a class you want to take. Ask the office worker questions. Write notes about the information you get from the office worker.

· How can I sign up for a class?
· Is there a fee?
· When does the class begin?

Talk About It

In a group, talk about the information you found for other adult classes in your town. Is there a class you want to take? Where is the class? What day or days is the class? What time? Is there a fee for the class? How can you sign up?

Wrap Up

Dolores and her friends are taking classes at an adult school. What kind of classes do you think an adult school should have? In a group, plan some classes students can take at a school. Make a schedule for five classes at the school. Choose classes that can help students at work, at home, and in the community. Decide the days and times for the classes, and write the information in a chart like the one below.

Class	Day	Time

Exchange schedules with another group. With a partner, role-play a conversation at the registration office of a school. One person is the student. One person is the office worker. Use the words in this unit, the present of **be**, past of **be, can,** and **can't**. For example:

A: Is there a math class on Monday evenings?

B: No, I'm sorry. The math class is on Tuesday and Thursday evenings.

A: Hmm. I can't take a class on Tuesday evening because I work that night. Can I take a computer class on Monday evenings?

B: Yes, you can. The computer class is from 6:00 to 9:00.

A: I want to sign up, please.

Practice your role-play. Then share it with the class.

Think About Learning

Check (✔) to show your learning in this unit. Then write one more thing you learned.

SKILLS / STRUCTURES	PAGE	EASY 😊	SO-SO 😐	DIFFICULT 😟
Talk about schools in the United States	2, 6			
Understand conversations about school	3, 7			
Use present of **be**	4			
Read and understand a sign at work	5			
Fill out an application for school	7			
Use past of **be**	8			
Use **can** and **can't**	9			
Read about and solve schedule problems	10			
Learn about adult schools in your community	12			

💡 📼 Scene 1: Conversation

With a partner, talk about the pictures. Listen to the conversation. Ask and answer the questions.

Jill and Chan worked all day. Now, it's time to go home.

Questions

How does Jill feel?

What are Jill's weekend plans?

Chan is surprised by Jill's plans. Why?

How do you relax?

Which do you think is more relaxing, many activities or one activity? Explain.

Vocabulary

Look at the words and pictures. Listen to your teacher. Say the words.

art museum

concert area

theater

gift shop

expensive

free

inexpensive

zoo

exhausted = very tired
to attend = to go to a class, concert, or play

to relax = to rest, to not work

to pick up

to have a picnic

to shop

Your Words

_____

_____

Exercise 1 Jill and her mother like to have picnics in the park. Look at the picture of the park Jill likes to visit on page 14. With a partner, talk about what she can do there. Circle the places that are inexpensive or free.

zoo   theater   art museum   (picnic area)

gift shop   science museum   concert area

Listening

Exercise 2 Listen to Jill talk about things she likes to do. Check (✓) the boxes next to the things she says she likes.

☐ Watch TV   ☐ Go to the zoo
☐ Visit an art or science museum   ☐ Watch a video
☐ Attend concerts or the theater   ☐ Shop at the mall
☐ Have a picnic   ☐ Play soccer
☐ Visit a science museum   ☐ Visit friends

After You Listen Compare your answers with a partner.

Your Turn

Circle the things you like to do in the list in Exercise 2. Add two more things you like to do. Share your answers with the class.

SPOTLIGHT on Review Simple Present

Affirmative Statements
I **work** on Sunday.
You **shop** at the mall.
He **likes** the zoo.
We **work** on Sunday
They **like** the zoo.

Add **-s** to the verb with he, she, and it.

Some verbs are irregular:
I **have** tickets to a concert.
She **has** tickets to a concert.

Questions
Do you **like** the zoo?
Does she **like** the zoo?

Negative Statements
I **don't work** on Sunday.
You **don't shop** at the mall.
She **doesn't like** the zoo.
We **don't work** on Sunday.
They **don't like** the zoo.

doesn't = does not
don't = do not

I **go** to the park on weekends.
He **goes** to the park in the morning.

Short Answers
Yes, I **do.**   No, I **don't.**
Yes, she **does.**   No, she **doesn't.**

Exercise 3 Read the story about Jill, her mother Peggy, and her boyfriend Alex. Complete the sentences. Write the correct word on the line. Use a form of the simple present.

On Saturdays Jill and her mother always **(1) go** _____ go _____ to the park.
They **(2) visit** _____ the art museum. Jill **(3) shop**
_____ at the gift shop. Peggy sometimes **(4) go**
_____ to the zoo, but Jill **(5) not go** _____ with her.
Peggy **(6) look** _____ at the animals there. On Saturday evenings Jill
and her boyfriend **(7) attend** _____ concerts. They usually **(8) not eat**
_____ at restaurants. Restaurants cost a lot of money.

Exercise 4 What do you do to relax? In your notebook, write sentences about you. Use the sentences in Exercise 3 to help you. For example, write "I usually visit my friends on the weekend." Then write sentences about your friends or family. For example, write "My father often goes to ball games."

Pair Work

Listen to the conversation between Jill and Chan. Then practice it with a partner.

Jill: What do you usually do on Saturdays to relax?

Chan: On Saturdays I watch sports on TV or listen to music. What do you do?

Jill: I always read the newspaper. Then I pick up my mother, and we go to the park. What do you do on Sundays?

Chan: On Sundays I like to have a picnic with my family.

Your Turn

Look at the conversation again. With a partner, make a new conversation. Use information about things you like to do on the weekends to relax. For example, ask "What do you do after class to relax?" "I always watch TV after class." Use the simple present. Share your conversation with the class.

Reading for Real

Jill brought a recreation center flyer to the office. Here is the information she read about programs in her community.

recreation
activities people like to do for fun

City Recreation Classes

Mexican Folk Dance
Classes in dances from different states in Mexico. Students will give a performance.
- Sat. 2:00–2:50 P.M.
- Adults only
- Fee: $14 for 8 weeks

Painting
Learn to paint nature and people. Dress in old clothes. Fee includes paper and paints.
- Wed. 4:30–5:20 P.M.
- 8 yrs.–18 yrs.
- Fee: $31 for 8 weeks

Judo
Self-defense techniques. Uniform necessary.
- Tue. 7:00–7:50 P.M.
- 5 yrs.–12 yrs.
- No fee

Swimming Lessons
Instruction for all skill levels, beginner through advanced. Loma Vista Pool.
- Tues. and Thurs. 7:00–8:00 P.M.
- 16 yrs. and over
- Fee: $23 for 10 lessons

Exercise 5 Jill read about recreation classes in her community. Read the questions below. Look for the answers in the flyer above. Circle the letter of the best answer.

1. Which class is for adults only?
   a. Mexican Folk Dance
   b. Judo
   c. Swimming Lessons

2. Which class meets two times a week?
   a. Mexican Folk Dance
   b. Swimming Lessons
   c. Painting

3. Chan wants to take judo. What does he need?
   a. self-defense
   b. old clothes
   c. a uniform

4. Which is the most expensive?
   a. Judo
   b. Swimming Lessons
   c. Painting

5. Can beginners take swimming lessons?
   a. yes
   b. no
   c. not sure

6. What does the fee for the drawing class include?
   a. old clothes
   b. paper and paint
   c. nature and people

Talk About It

In a group, ask and answer these questions. Why do people take recreation classes? In which classes can people exercise? Which recreational classes do you know about? Do you take recreation classes? Which classes do you want to take?

With a partner, talk about the pictures. Listen to the conversation. Ask and answer the questions.

Jill and Chan are at work on Friday afternoon.

Questions

What are Chan's plans for the evening?

What does the boss want?

Can Chan say no to his boss? Why or why not?

What do you do on Friday evenings?

Can you say no to your boss? Why? Why not?

Vocabulary

Look at the words and pictures. Listen to your teacher. Say the words.

Recreation Activities

to enjoy = to like

to go bowling

to jog

to play cards

to rent a video

to work out at the gym

Exercise 6 Which recreational activities are also kinds of exercise? Which activities cost money? Which activities can you do by yourself? Write the activities in the chart below. Use the words above to help you, or add your own ideas. Some words can go in more than one place.

Exercise	Cost money	Can do by yourself (alone)
jog		jog

Listening

Exercise 7 Listen to Jill and Chan talk about weekend activities. Check (✓) the activities Chan, his wife, and his son Ray like to do.

	Jog	Work out at the gym	Watch a video	Go bowling	Play hockey	Enjoy himself or herself
Chan	✓					
Chan's wife						
Ray						

After You Listen Compare your answers with a partner.

Talk About It

In a group, make a new chart. Follow the example of the chart in Exercise 7. At the top, each person writes one activity he or she does to relax. On the left, write the names of the people in your group. Talk about the activities. Make an X under the activities each person enjoys. Which activity do most people enjoy? Which activity do the fewest people enjoy?

SPOTLIGHT on Possessives

Chan's wife likes bowling.   The children's dog is here.   The boys' guitars are new.

Use 's to show that something belongs to someone.
Use s' if the word ends in s.

Possessive Adjectives

My dog is old. ⟶

Your dog is young. ⟶

His cards are new. ⟶

Her cards are old. ⟶

Its feet are dirty.

Our dog is black and white. ⟶

Their cards are new. ⟶

Possessive Pronouns

Mine is old.

Yours is young.

His are new.

Hers are old.

Ours is black and white.

Theirs are new.

Possessive adjectives are followed by a noun. Possessive pronouns are followed by a verb.
Correct: My dog is big. Mine is big.
Incorrect: Mine dog is big. My is big.

Exercise 8 Read the story about Chan's family. Complete the sentences below with a possessive form of the underlined words.

1. Chan and I go to the gym on the weekends. _____Our_____ gym is near the house.

2. Ray likes to play hockey. _____ team is very good.

3. Chan walks his dog in the morning. The _____ name is Lucky.

4. Chan's wife often volunteers at the school. _____ friends watch her coach soccer on Saturdays.

5. Ray and his friends eat lunch at a restaurant. _____ favorite restaurant is Duke's Burger Palace.

6. Do you like to eat at Duke's? What is _____ favorite restaurant?

Exercise 9 In your notebook, write five sentences about places you go and things you do to relax. Use the sentences in Exercise 8 to help you. Use possessives. For example, write "My house is near a park. My sister and I walk our dog there."

Talk About It

In a group, take turns talking about things in your classroom that belong to other students, and compare them to things you have. Use possessive adjectives and possessive pronouns. For example, say "Tam's pen is blue. Mine is black."

SPOTLIGHT on Reflexive Pronouns

Singular

I jog by **myself.**
You need to work by **yourself.**
He is teaching **himself** to play cards.
She walks by **herself.**

Plural

My wife and I jog by **ourselves.**
I hope you enjoy **yourselves** at the picnic.
The children are teaching **themselves**
to play cards.

Use **yourself** with one person and **yourselves** with two or more people.

By + reflexive means alone or without help.

Exercise 10 Chan's son, Ray, wrote a letter to his grandmother during summer vacation. Complete the sentences. Write the correct word on the line. Use reflexive pronouns.

June 1

Dear Grandma,

We're having a fun vacation. Every day we enjoy **(1)** _____ourselves_____ . Mom

walks by **(2)** _____ on the beach. She also goes by

(3) _____ to the mall. I am teaching **(4)** _____ to

play cards. Dad plays golf by **(5)** _____ . Mom and Dad hurt

(6) _____ playing tennis yesterday, but they're fine now. We are

really enjoying **(7)** _____ at the hotel. Come with us next time!

You can enjoy **(8)** _____ too!

Love, *Ray*

Exercise 11 In your notebook, write three sentences about things you like to do by yourself and three sentences about things your family members like to do by themselves. Use reflexive pronouns. For example, write, "I like to go to the beach by myself. My mother likes to shop by herself."

Pair Work

Listen to the conversation between Jill and Chan. Then practice it with a partner.

Jill: My mother is on vacation, and my boyfriend is busy. What can I do by myself this weekend?

Chan: Well, I like to jog by myself. And my wife likes to shop by herself. How about a movie? You can go to the movies by yourself.

Jill: I don't like to go to the movies by myself.

Chan: Really? I often go to the movies by myself. It's very relaxing.

Your Turn

With a partner, talk about things you like to do by yourself. Tell your partner three things you like to do alone. For example, say "I like to read by myself." Then listen to your partner and share your partner's information with the class.

Organizing Your Ideas

Jill and Chan enjoy many different recreational activities. Some things they do with friends or family members, and some they do by themselves. What activities do you do by yourself? What activities do you do with a friend or family member? What can you do by yourself or with a family member? Look at the recreational activities on pages 15 and 19, or think of other ideas. Then write the activities in the diagram below.

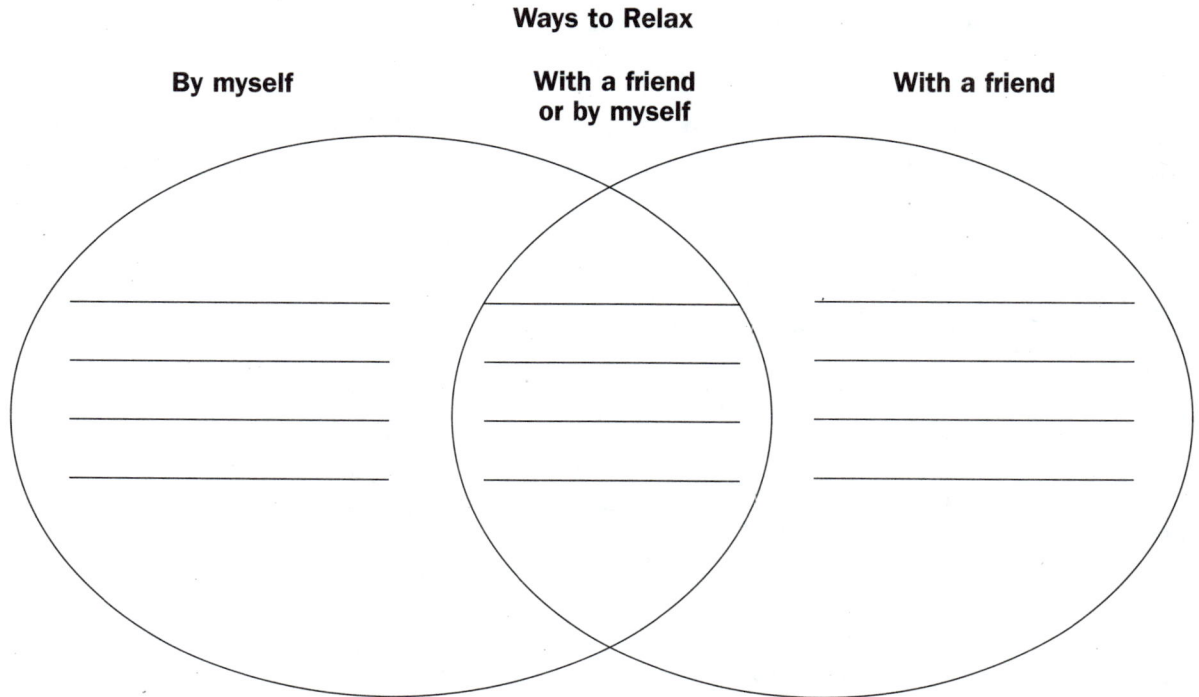

Ways to Relax

| | | |
| **By myself** | **With a friend or by myself** | **With a friend** |

_____   _____   _____
_____   _____   _____
_____   _____   _____
_____   _____   _____

Which activities in your diagram above are expensive? Which are inexpensive or free? Write your activities by cost in the diagram below.

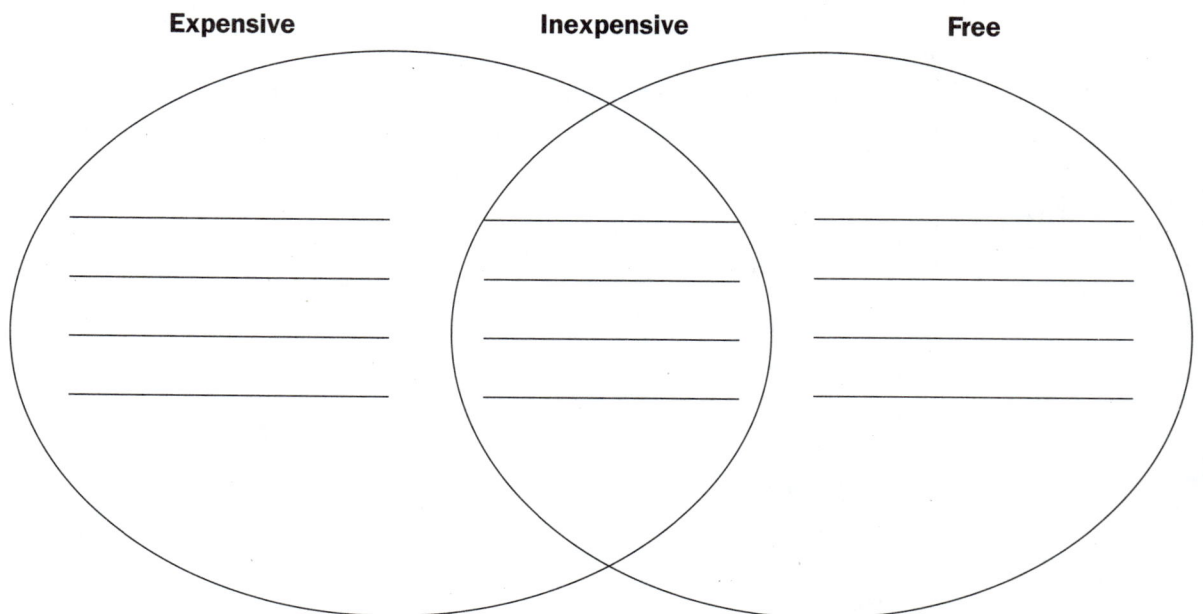

| | | |
| **Expensive** | **Inexpensive** | **Free** |

_____   _____   _____
_____   _____   _____
_____   _____   _____
_____   _____   _____

Talk About It

In a group, ask and answer questions about your lists. What inexpensive activities do you like? What do you like to do by yourself? What activities can you do with a friend?

Issues and Answers

Jill decided to write to Anita. Read the letter and Anita's advice. Then talk with other students about the advice. Do you agree? What other advice can you give?

Ask Abdul and Anita

DEAR ANITA,

I need help! I'm busy all the time. I love recreational activities with friends. I love to work out at the gym, go to concerts, and go bowling. But sometimes I need to relax alone. What relaxing activities can I do by myself? I don't want to spend a lot of money.

—JILL

DEAR JILL,

There are a lot of relaxing activities you can do by yourself. You can jog in the park or read books from the library. Those are free! Sometimes concerts in the park and museums are free for one day each week, too. Afternoon movies are usually inexpensive, if you go before 6:00 P.M. Find out the inexpensive times for movies, concerts, and museums. That can save you a lot of money.

—ANITA

Your Turn

Jill needs ideas for inexpensive activities. What kind of inexpensive activities do you enjoy?

Step 1: Work with a partner. Plan a fun weekend for you and your partner. You each have $20 to spend on your activities. Choose activities that are fun, inexpensive, and that you both enjoy. Look at your list on page 22 for ideas.

Step 2: Use your list to plan your weekend. What can you do in the morning? the afternoon? at night? Choose two activities for Saturday and two activities for Sunday.

Step 3: Share your plan with the class.

Community Involvement

In most communities, there are community recreation programs. These programs have different classes and activities both adults and children can enjoy. Sometimes the programs are in schools at night. Some communities have special buildings called community recreation centers.

Your Turn

With a partner, talk about community recreation programs. Do you know about the programs in your community? What classes can you take? List three classes or activities you are interested in.

1.

2.

3.

Community Action

Step 1: With a partner, choose one community recreation activity from your list above. Find out information about it. Ask an English speaker, use the telephone, the newspaper, or the Internet. Fill in the information below.

· Name of class or activity _____
· Place _____
· Dates and time of class _____
· Need to bring _____
· Fee _____

Step 2: With your partner, share your information with another pair of students. Tell them where and how you found the information.

Talk About It

In your group, talk about the classes and activities. Is there a class you want to enroll in? Which one? Why? If there is no class you want to take, explain the reason to your group.

Wrap Up

Jill and Chan relax in many different ways. Sometimes people like to relax and sometimes they like to be active. Organize recreational activities in the diagram below. Use activities on pages 15 and 19 for ideas, and add your own.

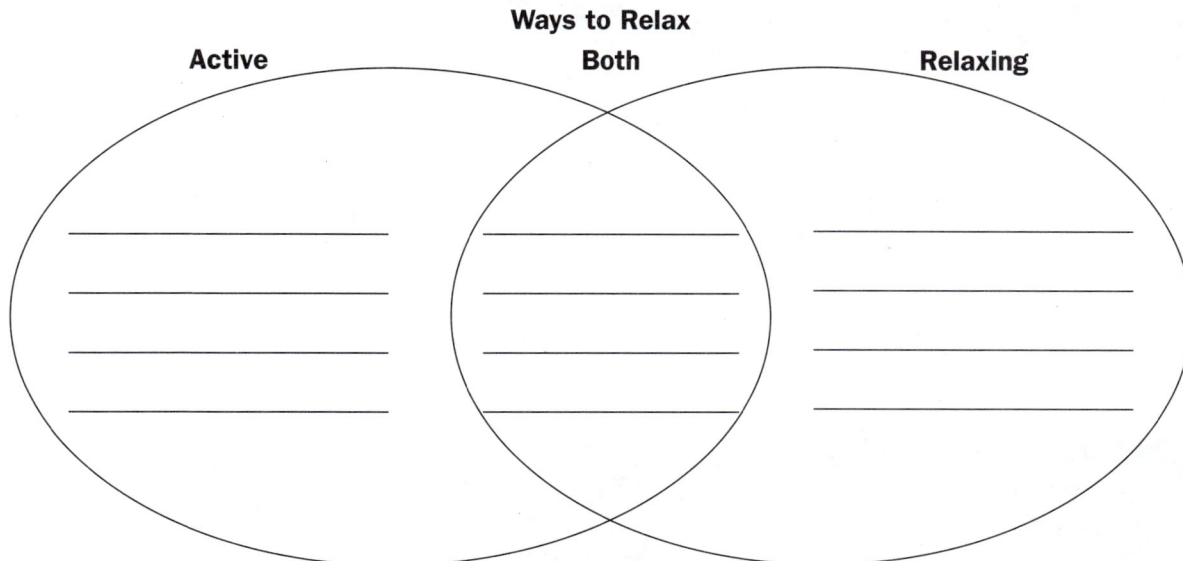

Ways to Relax

Active	Both	Relaxing

_____   _____   _____

_____   _____   _____

_____   _____

_____

With a partner, talk about recreational activities. Use the words in this unit, simple present, possessives, and reflexive pronouns. For example:

A: What do you like to do to relax?

B: I like to go to concerts in the park by myself. It's very relaxing.

A: Oh, I never go to concerts. They're expensive.

B: Not always. My park schedule says the concerts are free on Thursdays.

A: Really? That's great.

Practice your conversation. Then share it with the class.

Think About Learning

Check (✔) to show your learning in this unit. Then write one more thing you learned.

SKILLS / STRUCTURES	PAGE	EASY 😊	SO-SO 😐	DIFFICULT 😟
Talk about personal interests and plans	14, 18			
Complete an interest inventory	15			
Use simple present	16			
Read a schedule for recreational classes	17			
Understand conversations about plans and activities	19			
Use possessive nouns, pronouns, and adjectives	20			
Use reflexive pronouns	21			
Create a Venn diagram to organize your ideas	22			
Learn about recreation programs in your community	24			

💡 📼 Scene 1: Conversation

With a partner, talk about the pictures. Listen to the conversation. Ask and answer the questions.

Chan is in his kitchen. He sees a robbery happen outside his house. He calls 911.

Questions

Where is Chan?

What does Chan see happen?

Who does Chan call?

Are there a lot of problems with crime in your neighborhood?

Do you feel safe in your neighborhood? Why or why not?

Vocabulary

Look at the words and pictures. Listen to your teacher. Say the words.

  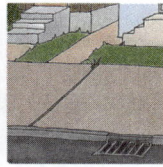    

| robbery | streetlight | sidewalk | thief | victim | to steal | to arrest |

emergency = serious problem that needs help right now
on the way = coming very soon

Your Words

_____

_____

Exercise 1 Read about the crime Chan saw. Complete the sentences. Use the words above to help you. Write the correct word on the line.

1. At 8:30 last night, Chan saw a _____robbery_____.

2. It was dark, but the _____ were on.

3. The _____ took the lady's purse and ran away.

4. Chan saw the _____. It was his neighbor, Maria.

5. He called 911 and told them there was an _____.

6. The police came, but they did not _____ the thief.

🎞 Listening

Exercise 2 Chan is listening to people talk about their old neighborhoods and their new neighborhoods. Write <u>yes</u> or <u>no</u> in the chart.

Name	Old Neighborhood Trees	Streetlights	Problems	New Neighborhood Trees	Streetlights	Problems
Issa	No	Yes	_____	_____	_____	_____
Maria	_____	_____	_____	_____	_____	_____
Jill	_____	_____	_____	_____	_____	_____

After You Listen Compare answers with a partner.

Your Turn

With a partner, ask and answer questions about things in your neighborhood. For example, ask "Where do you live?" "I live in Oak Ridge." "Are there trees in your neighborhood?" "Yes, I live near a park with a lot of trees."

SPOTLIGHT on There Was, There Were
Review There Is, There Are

Affirmative	Negative	Question/Answer
Present Singular		
There is a police station across the street.	**There isn't** a police station across the street.	**Is there** a police station across the street? Yes, **there is.**/No, **there isn't.**
Present Plural		
There are trees in front of the house.	**There aren't** any trees in front of the house.	**Are there** trees in front of the house? Yes, **there are.**/No, **there aren't.**
Past Singular		
There was a robbery last night.	**There wasn't** a robbery last night.	**Was there** a robbery last night? Yes, **there was.**/No, **there wasn't.**
Past Plural		
There were problems in my neighborhood last night.	**There weren't** any problems in my neighborhood last night.	**Were there** problems in your neighborhood last night? Yes, **there were.**/No, **there weren't.**

Exercise 3 Read about Chan's old neighborhood in China and about his new neighborhood. Complete the sentences. Write the correct word on the line. Use <u>there is</u>, <u>there are</u>, <u>there was</u>, <u>there were</u>.

Two years ago, Chan lived in a small village in China. **(1)** _____There were_____ small houses and friendly people in his neighborhood. **(2)** _____ a small market in the village. **(3)** _____ many trees and flowers.

Today Chan lives in a big city in the United States. In his neighborhood,

(4) _____ people from many different countries.

(5) not _____ a market in his neighborhood, but

(6) _____ a bus stop. Chan takes the bus to a big supermarket.

Exercise 4 In your notebook, write sentences about your old neighborhood in your native country and your new neighborhood in the United States. Use the sentences in Exercise 3 to help you. For example, write "I lived in a large city in Poland. There were many apartments there. Today I live in Baltimore. There are a lot of apartments here, too."

Pair Work

Listen to the conversation between Maria and Chan. Then practice it with a partner.

Maria: Were there streetlights in your old neighborhood in China?

Chan: No, there weren't.

Maria: Are there streetlights in your neighborhood now?

Chan: Yes, there are.

Your Turn

Look at the conversation again. With a partner, talk about your old and new neighborhoods. Talk about trees, streetlights, crime, and other things. Use **there is, there are, there was, there were.** Share your conversation with the class.

Reading for Real

Chan read a newspaper article about a man who solved a neighborhood problem.

One Man Who Changed a Neighborhood

When Mike Eagen and his wife, Ivette, bought their home on Guava Street in La Mesa, California, they were excited and proud. The neighborhood was clean and safe, and there were many trees. But Guava Street was near a freeway exit. The traffic was noisy and dangerous. Mike decided the street needed a stop sign and speed bumps.

First, he looked in the phone book for numbers for government offices in the city of La Mesa. He called all the offices until he found someone to help him. Her name was Kathy Feilen.

Kathy sent Mike some papers. They explained how to ask for speed bumps, stop signs, or other things to make the neighborhood safe. Then Mike asked his neighbors to sign a letter asking for speed bumps.

He sent the letter to the City Council. He visited town meetings, and he called City Council members. Some of them came to his house to look at the traffic problem. One night Mike spoke to a large group of people at a City Council meeting.

Eight months later, city workers put speed bumps and a stop sign on Guava Street. Now the neighborhood is safe and quiet. Everyone thanked Mike Eagen for his hard work.

speed bumps
bumps in the road to make people drive slowly

Exercise 5 Mike made a big difference in his neighborhood. Read the questions below. Look for the answers in the article above. Circle the letter of the best answer.

1. How did Mike and Ivette Eagen feel when they moved to Guava Street?
   a. excited and proud
   b. clean and safe
   c. noisy and dangerous

2. What was the big problem in the neighborhood?
   a. traffic
   b. quiet
   c. a lot of trees

3. How did Mike want to solve the problem?
   a. move
   b. ask for speed bumps and stop signs
   c. take the freeway

4. Who does Kathy Feilen work for?
   a. the city council
   b. the City of La Mesa
   c. Mike

5. What did Kathy send Mike?
   a. speed bumps
   b. papers
   c. a letter

6. What happened eight months later?
   a. Mike spoke at a city council meeting.
   b. City workers put up speed bumps and a stop sign.
   c. The neighbors signed a letter.

Talk About It

In a group, ask and answer these questions.
Is there a problem with traffic in your neighborhood? Are there other problems in your neighborhood? Do you talk to your neighbors about these problems?

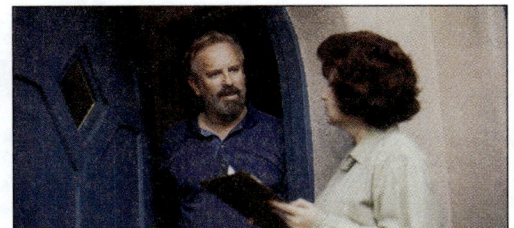

With a partner, talk about the pictures. Listen to the conversation. Ask and answer the questions.

Chan decides to ask his neighbors to help solve the problems with crime in the neighborhood.

I'm Issa, and I'm worried too. Let's organize a Neighborhood Watch Program.

Hi, I'm Chan. I live in the house next to yours. I'm concerned about the crime problems in our neighborhood.

A man stole my purse.

There's a big problem with graffiti in this neighborhood.

We need to do something about the traffic problem.

I have a car alarm, but a thief broke into my car and took my radio.

Councilman Smith, can you help us with these problems?

I live in this neighborhood too. I promise to work with you and do something to solve these problems.

Chan

Councilman Smith

Questions

What are Chan and his neighbors talking about at the Neighborhood Watch meeting?
What happened to Maria? What happened to Jill?

Are there problems in your neighborhood?
Do you know about a Neighborhood Watch group in your neighborhood?

Vocabulary

Look at the words and pictures. Listen to your teacher. Say the words.

alarm

city council member

concerned

graffiti

to break into

to organize

to promise

to solve a problem

to happen = to take place

Neighborhood Watch = group of neighbors that watch the neighborhood and call the police if there is a problem

to do something about

to change or fix the problem

Exercise 6 Chan heard these words at the meeting. Circle the letter of the phrase that best completes each sentence.

1. Chan's neighbors are **concerned** about crime. They are
   a. sad about it.
   b. worried about it.
   c. happy about it.

2. Chan and Issa **organized** a Neighborhood Watch meeting. They
   a. planned and prepared for it.
   b. reported about it.
   c. talked about it.

3. A thief **breaks into** Jill's car. He
   a. drives the car very fast.
   b. stops the car quickly.
   c. breaks a window to get into the car.

4. A **city council member**
   a. talks to his neighbors.
   b. cleans the city streets.
   c. works for people in the city to solve problems.

5. Councilman Smith **promises** to do something about the problem. He
   a. thinks about the problem.
   b. agrees to solve the problem.
   c. asks questions about the problem.

6. **Graffiti** is
   a. a painting in a museum.
   b. words or pictures painted on buildings without permission.
   c. a traffic sign.

Listening

Exercise 7 Listen to Chan's neighbors talk about the problems in their neighborhood. What happened? When? Take notes. Do not write sentences; only write important words.

After You Listen Compare answers with a partner.

Victim	Problem	When
Maria	thief stole purse	last Friday night
Issa		
Jill		

Your Turn

With a partner, ask and answer questions about the information in the chart above.
For example, ask, "What happened to Maria?" "A thief stole her purse last Friday night."

SPOTLIGHT on Review Simple Past

Affirmative

I **waited** for the bus.
You **helped** your neighbor.
He **stayed** until the police arrived.

We **tried** to help.

The policemen **stopped** the car.

Negative

They **didn't wait** for the bus.
He **didn't call** the police.

Question
Did you **wait** for the bus?

To make the past tense with regular verbs, add **-ed** to the **base form** of the verb.

Some verbs that end in **y** change to **i** before the **-ed** is added.

Some verbs double the final letter when **-ed** is added.

To make the negative past, use **didn't** followed by the base form of the verb. Do not add **-s** to the base form for **he** and **she**.

Short Answer
Yes, I **did.** / No, I **didn't.**

---

b a r k

Exercise 8 Read about the problem Chan had in his neighborhood. Complete the sentences. Write the correct word on the line. Use the simple past form of the verbs.

Chan and his family **(1) live** _____lived_____ in a small village in China. Then they **(2) move** _____ into a nice neighborhood in a big city in California five years ago. They **(3) rent** _____ a house on Elm Street. They **(4) like** _____ their neighbors, but they **(5) not like** _____ their neighbors' dog. It **(6) not stay** _____ inside at night. It **(7) bark** _____ all night every night outside. Finally, Chan and his neighbors **(8) talk** _____ to the owners of the dog. They **(9) promise** _____ to keep the dog inside at night. The neighbors **(10) thank** _____ the owners. Now the neighborhood is quiet at night and all the neighbors are happy.

Exercise 9 In your notebook, write sentences about your first neighborhood in the United States. Use the sentences in Exercise 8 to help you. When did you move into the neighborhood? What did you like about the neighborhood? What didn't you like? Did you talk to other neighbors about problems in the neighborhood?

Your Turn

With a partner, ask and answer questions about your first neighborhood in the United States. Use the sentences in Exercise 9 to help you. For example, ask, "Did you move into a quiet neighborhood?" "No, I didn't. I moved into a noisy neighborhood."

SPOTLIGHT on Simple Simple Past with Irregular Verbs

Affirmative	Negative	
I **bought** an alarm for my car.	I **didn't buy** a radio for my car.	Irregular past verbs do not have **-ed** endings. The past form is a different word.
The dog **ran** after the thief.	The dog **didn't run** after the cat.	
The officer **drove** to the park.	The officer **didn't drive** to the park.	Use **didn't** and the **base form** of the verb to make the negative past.
The police **found** the purse.	They **didn't find** the thief.	Verbs are always regular in the negative past.

Questions		
Did you **go** to school?	Yes, **I did.** / No, **I didn't.**	Use **did** and the **base form** of the verb to ask questions in the past.
Did he **steal** your purse?	Yes, **he did.** / No, **he didn't.**	

break	broke	get	got	say	said
come	came	give	gave	steal	stole
do	did	hear	heard	take	took
eat	ate	think	thought	write	wrote

Exercise 10 Maria talks about the night a thief stole her purse. Complete the sentences. Write the correct word on the line. Use regular and irregular past verbs.

Last Friday night was a bad night. I **(1) go** _____ went _____ to the store and

(2) buy _____ some food. I **(3) not come** _____ home

until about 8:00. A man **(4) run** _____ up behind me and **(5) steal**

_____ my purse. A nice neighbor **(6) call** _____ the

police. They **(7) come** _____ quickly, but they **(8) not find**

_____ my purse or the thief.

Exercise 11 In your notebook, write about a day in your past. You can write about a good day, a bad day or a usual day. Use five or more past verbs in your sentences. Try to use the negative past in some of the sentences.

Pair Work

Listen to the conversation between the police officer and Maria. Then practice it with a partner.

Police: What time did you come home?

Maria: I came home about 8:00.

Police: Did you see the thief?

Maria: No, I didn't. He ran up behind me. I fell down and hurt my head.

Talk About It

In a group, read the stories you wrote for Exercise 11. Ask and answer questions about what people in your group wrote. For example, ask, "Did you get up at 6:00?" "Yes, I did. I got up at 6:00." "Did you get up at 7:00?" "No, I didn't. I ate breakfast at 7:00."

Organizing Your Ideas

an attractive neighborhood

Chan wants to make his neighborhood a good place to live. Think about things that make a neighborhood a good place to live. What makes a neighborhood safe? What makes it attractive? What are some other things that make a neighborhood a good place to live? Write your ideas in the chart below.

Things that make a neighborhood safe	Things that make a neighborhood attractive	Other things that make a neighborhood a good place to live
police station speed bumps	clean streets	swimming pool

Now think about your neighborhood. What do you like about your neighborhood? Are there any problems? Make a list of the good things in your neighborhood. Then make a list of the things you don't like.

Things I like about my neighborhood	Things I don't like about my neighborhood

Talk About It

In a group, talk about your lists. What do you think makes a neighborhood a good place to live? What makes your neighborhood a good neighborhood? What do you want to change about your neighborhood?

Issues and Answers

Chan decided to ask Anita for advice about making his neighborhood safe. Read the letter and Anita's advice. Then talk with other students about the advice. Do you agree? What other advice can you give?

Ask Abdul and Anita

DEAR ANITA,

I like my neighborhood. It's a nice place to live. But the people in the house across the street are a problem for everyone in the neighborhood. Every weekend they have loud parties. Sometimes they don't end until 2:00 A.M. I think there is a lot of drinking at the parties and maybe some drugs too. I'm worried about the safety of our neighborhood, and I want a good night's sleep. What can I do?

—CHAN

DEAR CHAN,

There are many things you can do. Talk to the people across the street. Sometimes people don't know you can hear them. If they aren't quiet after you talk with them and it's late at night, call the police. They can tell your neighbors to be more quiet. They can also arrest your neighbors if someone has drugs or a young person is drinking at their house. Good luck.

—ANITA

Your Turn

Chan is thinking about moving to a different neighborhood. He wants to make sure there are no big problems in his new neighborhood. Help Chan think about some neighborhood problems, and then decide what he can look for in a new neighborhood to make sure he doesn't have big problems in his new neighborhood.

Step 1: Work with a partner. Look again at all the pages you studied in this unit (pages 26 to 34) to find the different problems that sometimes happen in neighborhoods. Also look at the list you made on page 34 about the things you don't like in your own neighborhood. Make a list of the problems in some neighborhoods in your notebook. For example, write "a lot of traffic."

Step 2: Think about things to look for in a new neighborhood to solve these problems. Write the solution next to the problem in your notebook. For example, next to "a lot of traffic" write, "stop signs."

Step 3: Share your ideas with the class.

Community Involvement

The people in city government want to help people in their community. It's important for you to write or call them when there is a problem in your neighborhood. They need information to help solve neighborhood problems.

Your Turn

With a partner, talk about the people in your city government. Do you know the name of your mayor? Do you know any other people in your city government? What do they do?

Community Action

Step 1: With a partner, learn about the people in your city government. Call the mayor's office or other office in the city government or use the Internet. Find the answers to these questions.

Who is the mayor of your city? _____

Who are the members of your city council? _____

_____

_____

_____

One city council member lives in your community. He or she works to solve problems in your neighborhood. Find that person's name, office phone number, and address. Write this information below.

_____

_____

_____

Step 2: Work with a group of students from your neighborhood. Write a letter to your city council member about a problem in your neighborhood, and about your idea to help solve it. All the students in your class who live in the neighborhood can sign the letter. Each student needs to write his or her first and last name and address on the letter. Send the letter to your city council member. Use the address of your school for the return address. Maybe your council member will write back!

Talk About It

In a group, share your letters and the other information you found in Step 1. Who is the city council person from your area? How did you find the information? Did your group send a letter to someone in the city government? What did you say in the letter?

💡 Wrap Up

What makes a neighborhood a good place to live? Work in a group, and decide what a neighborhood needs. Choose three things that make a neighborhood safe, three things that make a neighborhood attractive, and three other things that make a neighborhood a nice place to live. Everyone should agree on the lists. Write your ideas in the chart below.

Things that make a neighborhood safe	Things that make a neighborhood attractive	Other things that make a neighborhood a good place to live
1.	1.	1.
2.	2.	2.
3.	3.	3.

Choose a partner from a different group. Do not look at your partner's list. Ask questions about your partner's neighborhood. Use words from this unit, regular and irregular past, and **there is / there are / there was / there were.** For example:

A: Are there speed bumps in your neighborhood?

B: No there aren't. We didn't put speed bumps in our neighborhood.

A: Did you build a police station?

B: Yes, we did. We built a police station.

A: You made a safe neighborhood.

Now tell the class about your partner's neighborhood.

Think About Learning

Check (✔) to show your learning in this unit. Then write one more thing you learned.

SKILLS / STRUCTURES	PAGE	EASY 😊	SO-SO 😐	DIFFICULT 🙁
Talk about crime problems in a neighborhood	26, 30			
Understand conversations about neighborhood problems	27, 31			
Use **there is/are/was/were**	28			
Read a story about neighbors who solved a neighborhood problem	29			
Use regular past	32			
Use irregular past	33			
Create a table to organize your ideas	34			
Write a letter about a neighborhood problem	35			
Learn about local government in your community	36			

Unit 4 Time Cards and Paychecks

💡 📼 ## Scene 1: Conversation

**With a partner, talk about the pictures. Listen to the conversation.
Ask and answer the questions.**

Mario and Yoko work at Evanston Electronics. Yoko is an office worker. She started her job at the company yesterday. She needs to punch in at the time clock.

> What did I do wrong? I can't get this time clock to work.

> Maybe I can help you. How did you hold your time card?

> This way.

> You can turn the card, like this. When did you start to work here?

> Yesterday. I am a new employee. I work the day shift. Thanks so much for your help!

> Sure, no problem. See you around.

no problem
I'm happy to do it, it isn't a problem for me.

Questions

When did Yoko start to work at Evanston Electronics?

What is Yoko's problem?

How do you think Yoko feels?

Do you use a time clock?

What was your first day at work or school like?

Vocabulary

Look at the words and pictures. Listen to your teacher. Say the words.

| day shift | night shift | swing (or second) shift | time card | to punch in | to punch out |

overtime = more work hours than a regular day or week
to earn = to receive money for work

Your Words

_____

_____

Exercise 1 Yoko and Mario work different shifts at Evanston Electronics. Complete the sentences. Use the words above to help you. Write the correct word on the line.

Yoko is a new employee at Evanston Electronics. She needs to

(1) _____ when she comes to work, and **(2)** _____

when she leaves. She works the **(3)** _____ from 8:00 A.M. to 4:00 P.M.

Mario comes to work at 4:00 P.M. and works the **(4)** _____ until

midnight. When Mario works more than 40 hours a week, he works

(5) _____ He likes **(6)** _____ extra money.

Listening

Exercise 2 Mario is telling Yoko about his work schedule. Listen to their conversation and complete the chart.

After You Listen Add up the total hours per day that **Mario worked.** Then add up the total hours Mario worked in a week. Compare answers with a partner.

Your Turn

With a partner, ask and answer questions about Mario's schedule, and your schedule. For example, ask, "When did Mario work?" "He worked Sunday through Friday. He didn't work Wednesday."

Evanston Electronics Time Card

Employee: Mario Gonzalez

Day	IN	OUT	Hours per day
Sun			
Mon	4:00		
Tues		12:00	
Wed			
Thurs		12:00	
Fri	4:00		
Sat			
Hours per week			

SPOTLIGHT on Review Information Questions in the Past

Questions			Answers
Who	did	Yoko call?	She **called Sue.**
When	did	Yoko punch in?	She punched in **at 8:00.**
Where	did	she find the time card?	She found it **on the table.**
What	did	they do yesterday?	**They worked.**
Which time card	did	Yoko use?	She used **the small one.**
Why	did	she arrive late?	She was late **because she missed the bus.**
How	did	Yoko learn to punch in?	**Mario helped her.**

Use **did** + base form of the verb with **wh-** question words to make past tense questions.

Exercise 3 Yoko likes her new job. Complete the sentences. Write the correct question on the line. Make information questions in the past.

1. (Yoko / go) **to her job** _____ *Where did Yoko go?* _____

2. (Yoko / leave her house) **at 7:30 a.m.** _____?

3. (Yoko / punch in) **at 8:00 a.m.** _____?

4. (Yoko / ask for help) **Mario** _____?

5. (Yoko and Sue / go for lunch) **to the deli** _____?

6. (Mario / miss work) **because he was sick** _____?

Exercise 4   In your notebook, write information questions about the past to ask a partner. For example, write, "Where did you go yesterday? Who did you eat lunch with yesterday?" Ask your partner the questions. Then answer your partner's questions.

Pair Work

Listen to the conversation between Mario and Yoko. Then practice it with a partner.

Yoko: What shift did you work last week?

Mario: I worked the swing shift. I punched in at 4:00 p.m. every day. How about you?

Yoko: I worked the day shift all week. Do you always work the swing shift?

Mario: Yes, I do. But sometimes I stay late. I like to work overtime to earn more money.

Talk About It

In a group, talk about work you do at a job or at home. Use information questions in the past. For example, "What did you do yesterday?" "I cleaned my house." "When did you take a break?" "I didn't take a break. I worked all day."

Reading for Real

Yoko got her first paycheck. She reads the information on the paycheck stub, and is trying to understand the deductions. Deductions are the money that the company took out of Yoko's paycheck.

Evanston Electronics		Pay period beginning	03/03
3244 Main Street	Date **March 27**	Pay period ending	03/11
Centerville, CA 92443		Rate	$ 8.50
		Hours	40
Pay to **Yoko Tanaka** $ **285.40**		GROSS PAY	$340.00
		FEDERAL TAX	$ 27.00
two hundred eightyfive and 40/100 dollars		STATE TAX	$ 2.86
		SOCIAL SECURITY	$ 19.84
Tom Evanston		MEDICARE	$ 4.90
		NET PAY	$285.40

Exercise 5 Yoko needs to understand the deductions. Read the questions below. Look for the answers in the paycheck above. Circle the letter of the best answer.

1. What was Yoko's gross pay?
   a. $285.40
   b. $340.00
   c. $270.00

2. How much did she pay in federal taxes?
   a. $27.00
   b. $19.84
   c. $4.90

3. How much did she pay for Medicare?
   a. $4.90
   b. $2.86
   c. $19.84

4. How much did she pay in state taxes?
   a. $4.90
   b. $19.84
   c. $2.86

5. What did she pay for Social Security?
   a. $19.84
   b. $2.86
   c. $4.90

6. What was Yoko's net pay?
   a. $340.00
   b. $270.00
   c. $285.40

Talk About It

In a group, ask and answer these questions. Do you have a job? How often do you get a paycheck? Does your company take out the same deductions as Yoko's company? Do you think workers pay too much money in taxes?

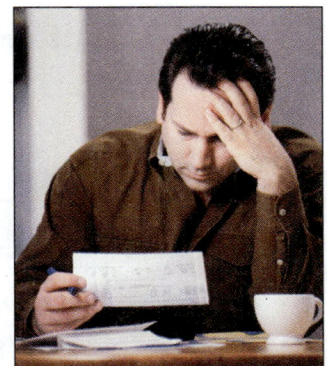

Scene 2: Conversation

With a partner, talk about the pictures. Listen to the conversation.
Ask and answer the questions.

Mario looks at his paycheck. He thinks there's a mistake.

I can't figure out this paycheck. I had four hours of overtime last week, but there's no extra pay for the extra hours.

And the overtime rate of pay is a lot more than the regular rate. Maybe you can ask your supervisor about the paycheck error.

Pay period beginning	March 3
Pay period ending	March 11
Rate	$ 10.00
Hours	40
GROSS PAY	$400.00
FEDERAL TAX	$ 28.00
STATE TAX	$ 3.40
SOCIAL SECURITY	$ 22.00
MEDICARE	$ 6.20
NET PAY	$340.40

I was thinking about that. This is the second mistake in my paycheck. It happened a few months ago too. I know I need to say something, but I don't want Mr. Evanston to fire me!

Questions

What are Yoko and Mario talking about?

What's Mario's problem?

What does Yoko think Mario can do about the problem?

Do you think Mario will talk to Mr. Evanston? Explain your answer.

Did you ever have an error on your paycheck? What did you do about it?

Vocabulary

Look at the words and pictures. Listen to your teacher. Say the words.

deductions = money a company takes out of a paycheck
federal taxes = money workers pay to the U.S. government
gross pay = amount of money a worker earns before deductions
Medicare = government plan that pays for medical expenses for older people
pay stub = part of paycheck that tells how much workers earned and what their deductions were
rate = how much a worker earns per hour
Social Security = government plan to give money each month to older people who don't work

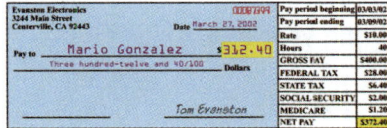

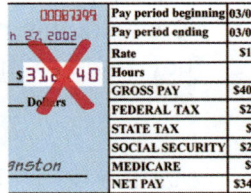

net pay = money a worker
receives after deductions

pay period

**(a paycheck)
error**

employees

**to fire an
employee**

**to figure
out**

Exercise 6 Mario and Yoko are reading their pay stubs. Match the meanings in Column B with the words in Column A. Write the letter.

COLUMN A	COLUMN B
__f__ 1. deductions	a. government plan that pays for medical expenses for people who are older and don't work
_____ 2. gross pay	b. money the worker receives after the company takes money for taxes and other things out of the paycheck
_____ 3. federal taxes	c. money workers pay to the U.S. government
_____ 4. net pay	d. the total amount of money a worker earns before the company takes out money for taxes and other things
_____ 5. medicare	e. money a worker earns for each hour of work
_____ 6. rate	f. taxes and other money the company takes out of money the worker earned

Listening

Exercise 7 Listen to Mario talk to Mr. Evanston about his paycheck. As he speaks, fill in the paycheck below.

Evanston Electronics 3244 Main Street Centerville, CA 92443 Date __March 27__ Pay to __Mario Gonzalez__ $_____ _____ dollars __Tom Evanston__	Pay period ending	03/11
	Rate	$10.00
	Hours	
	GROSS PAY	
	FEDERAL TAX	$28.00
	STATE TAX	$3.40
	SOCIAL SECURITY and MEDICARE	$28.20
	NET PAY	

After You Listen Compare answers with a partner. Then fill in the net pay on Mario's paycheck.

Your Turn

With a partner, ask and answer questions about Mario's paycheck. For example, say, "How much money did Mario earn in gross pay?" "He earned $ _____." "How much did Mario pay in state taxes? He paid $_____ in state taxes."

SPOTLIGHT on Past Time Words

Yesterday	**Last**
You went to work **yesterday morning.**	I talked to my boss **last night.**
Yesterday afternoon he worked overtime.	**Last week** you worked 40 hours.
We worked overtime **yesterday evening.**	He didn't receive the correct pay **last month.**

Ago
I arrived **five minutes ago.**
He started his new job **two days ago.**
They came to the United States **one year ago.**

Past time words can come at the beginning of the sentence or at the end of the sentence, but not in the middle.
Incorrect: I went yesterday to work.

Exercise 8 Mario and Yoko were busy last month. Complete the sentences. Write the correct word on the line. Use <u>yesterday</u>, <u>last</u> or <u>ago</u>.

1. Mario worked overtime _____ *last* _____ night.

2. Yoko started her new job two weeks _____.

3. _____ Friday Mario got his paycheck.

4. Yoko came to the United States _____ year.

5. Mario ate lunch an hour _____.

6. _____ evening Yoko went to English class.

Exercise 9 In your notebook, write sentences about things you did in the past. Use past time words. What did you do yesterday? What did you do last year? What did you do two hours ago?

Talk About It

In a group, ask and answer questions about things you did in the past. Use the examples in the grammar box above and the sentences you wrote in Exercise 9 to help you. For example, ask, "What did you do last Saturday night?" "I worked." "When did you start your job?" "I started my job a year ago."

SPOTLIGHT on Past Progressive

Affirmative Statements

I **was working** at 7:30 this morning.

You **were working** the day shift.

She **was punching in** when the boss arrived.

We **were eating** lunch when the phone rang.

They **were punching out** at 8:00.

Negative Statements

I **wasn't sleeping** at 7:30.

You **weren't working** the night shift.

She **wasn't taking** a break.

We **weren't eating** dinner.

They **weren't punching in** at 8:00.

was not = wasn't were not = weren't

To make the past progressive, use the past form of **be** followed by the verb and **-ing**

Questions

Were you **working** at 7:30?

Was she **punching in** when the boss arrived?

Were they **eating** lunch?

Short Answers

Yes, I **was.** / No, I **wasn't.**

Yes, she **was.** / No, she **wasn't.**

Yes, they **were.** / No, they **weren't.**

Use the past progressive to talk about an action that was continuing at a certain time in the past or at the time another action happened. The time that the action started or ended is not important.

Exercise 10 Read about the activities of Mario and Yoko. Complete the sentences. Write the correct word on the line. Use the past progressive form of the words in the parenthesis ( ).

1. At 7:00 yesterday morning, Mario (**not sleep**) ___wasn't sleeping___.

2. He (**eat**) _____ breakfast at 7:00.

3. At 7:30, he (**drive**) _____ to work.

4. He (**punch in**) _____ when Yoko arrived.

5. Yoko and Mario (**not eat**) _____ lunch at 10:30. They (**work**)

    _____.

Exercise 11 In your notebook, write six sentences about your activities yesterday and the times at which you were doing them. Begin with the time you were eating breakfast, and end with the time you were sleeping. Use the sentences in Exercise 10 to help you.

Pair Work

Listen to the conversation between Yoko and Mario. Then practice it with a partner.

Yoko: Why were you meeting with your supervisor?

Mario: I was showing him my paystub from last week.

Yoko: Why were you showing him your paystub?

Mario: I worked overtime last week. We were trying to figure out my overtime pay.

Your Turn

With a partner, ask and answer questions about what you were doing yesterday. Use the sentences you wrote in Exercise 11 to help you. For example, "Were you working at 8:00 last night?" "Yes, I was working at 8:00 last night."

Organizing Your Ideas

day planner

> THINGS TO DO
>
> call Dr. Lee
> buy groceries
> go to bank

Yoko had a busy day at work yesterday. Her boss, Mr. Evanston, changed the time of his meeting with the supervisors from 3:00 P.M. to 2:00 P.M. There were a lot of things Mr. Evanston wanted Yoko to do before the meeting, and she had some other work to finish. Yoko made a list. She wrote the most important tasks at the top of the page, and the less important tasks at the bottom. Read the tasks below. What do you think she did first? What did she do second and third? Fill in Yoko's planner. Write the activities in the same order you think she wrote them.

make copies of Mr. Evanston's report for the meeting
deliver the mail
type Mr. Evanston's report for the meeting
order Mr. Evanston's plane tickets for his trip next month
pick up the mail
email the supervisors about the change in the meeting time
send a fax to the bank
order doughnuts and coffee for the meeting
schedule a meeting with Mr. Brown next week

DAY PLANNER

Tuesday, November 12

8:00 _____
9:00 _____
10:00 _____
11:00 _____
12:00 _____
1:00 _____
2:00 _____
3:00 _____
4:00 _____
5:00 _____

In your notebook, make a list of the important things you need to do this week. List activities at your job or chores at home. Fill in the planner below. Prioritize your activities. Write the most important activities at the top.

DAY PLANNER

Monday _____
_____
Tuesday _____
_____
Wednesday _____
_____
Thursday _____
_____
Friday _____
_____

Talk About It

In a group, ask and answer questions about your planners. What is the most important thing you have to do? Why?

Issues and Answers

Yoko's friend Ivan is trying to figure out his overtime. Read the letter and Mr. Nakamura's advice. Then talk with other students about the advice. Do you agree? What other advice can you give?

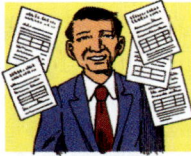

Ask Mr. Nakamura

MR. NAKAMURA,

I have a new job. I have lots of work to do. Sometimes I work overtime. I don't understand the rules about overtime. On Thursday last week I worked one hour of overtime. In all, I worked a total of 40 hours last week, but I didn't get extra money for my hour of overtime on my paycheck. Also, what happens if I work on a weekend or a holiday? Do I get extra pay?

—IVAN

DEAR IVAN,

There is a federal law about overtime. The name of the law is the Fair Labor Standards Act. The law says that employers must pay extra money per hour of overtime to employees who work more than 40 hours in one week. They do not have to pay extra money when the person works more than 8 hours in one day. Some small businesses don't need to follow the rule.

The law says that overtime pay is one and a half times the employee's regular pay. Do employers pay extra for special days? No, employers don't have to pay extra for Saturdays, Sundays, and holidays. They only must pay extra when the employees work more than 40 hours.

Good luck with your new job!

—MR. NAKAMURA, HUMAN RESOURCES MANAGER

Your Turn

Figure out the correct amount of money to pay Ivan for her work.

Step 1: Work in groups of three. Figure out Ivan's gross pay for her last paycheck. He worked 40 hours at her regular pay of $8.00 per hour and six hours overtime at $12.00 per hour. How much was his gross pay?

Step 2: Now figure out Ivan's deductions. The company takes out 10% of gross pay for federal taxes, 1 % of gross pay for state taxes and 7% of gross pay for Social Security and Medicare together. How much money did the company take out of Ivan's check for each deduction?

Step 3: Finally, figure out Ivan's net pay. Add the cost of all the taxes from Step 2 and subtract that number from his gross pay from Step 1. Compare your answers with another group. Do both groups have the same answers ?

Community Involvement

Businesses have different ways to pay their employees. Some companies give paychecks every week, some pay their workers every two weeks, and some pay once a month. Businesses also have different ways to take out deductions from employees' paychecks. Some companies take deductions to help the worker have more money for retirement. Other companies take money out of the paychecks for health insurance for the employee. Most companies pay employees extra money for overtime hours, but some do not.

Your Turn

With a partner, talk about pay in your native country. Do people get paychecks? Do companies take out taxes? Is it the same as or different from the United States?

Community Action

Step 1: Interview a classmate or friend about his or her workplace. Find the answers to these questions. Write them in your notebook.

Where do you work?

How does your company count the hours the employees work? (timeclock? other?)

How often does your company give paychecks?

Does your company pay employees for overtime? Why or why not?

What deductions does your company take out of the workers' paychecks?

Step 2: In a group of four, talk about the information you learned in the interview. In your notebook, write the group's answers to these questions.

How many companies use timeclocks?

How many companies give paychecks every week?

How many companies pay overtime?

Do all the companies take out the same deductions? How are they different?

Talk About It

In a group, ask and answer these questions about the information you learned.
Which companies are good places to work? Is there a company you want to work for? Why?

💡 Wrap Up

Mario and Yoko sometimes work overtime to help pay their bills. Do you have time to work overtime to earn some extra money" Write the schedule you have now in the calendar below. Write **work, school,** or **family** in the boxes below to show the times you are busy.

	Sun	Mon	Tues	Weds	Thurs	Thurs	Fri	Sat
Morning 9:00–12:00								
Afternoon 2:00–5:00								
Evening 6:00–9:00								

With a partner, talk about your schedule. One student is the supervisor, and needs employees to work overtime next week. One student is the employee. Use the schedule you made above to tell your supervisor the times you can work. Write **OT** in the chart for the times you decide to work overtime. For example:

A: I need people to work overtime next week. Can you work Monday through Friday from 6:00 to 9:00?

B: I have to go to computer class on Tuesday night, but I can work the other nights.

A: OK, you can work four nights next week for a total of twelve hours of overtime. Is that right?

B: That's right. Thank you for the overtime.

Practice your conversation. Then share it with the class.

Think About Learning

Check (✔) to show your learning in this unit. Then write one more thing you learned.

SKILLS / STRUCTURES	PAGE	EASY 😊	SO-SO 😐	DIFFICULT 😞
Talk about timecards, work schedules, and paychecks	38, 42			
Understand conversations about time cards and paychecks	39, 43			
Use information questions in the past	40			
Read a paycheck stub	41			
Fill out a paycheck	41, 43			
Use past time words	44			
Talk about things you did in the past	44, 45			
Use the past progressive	45			
Learn about company pay practices in your community	48			

Unit 5   Shape Up!

Scene 1: Conversation

**With a partner, talk about the pictures. Listen to the conversation.
Ask and answer the questions.**

Henri and Mark are at work.

I need to lose some weight. What can I do?

Henri, you need to exercise. Can you ride your bicycle to work?

No, I can't. I sold it.

CHARGE
SAVE 10% TODAY!

You can hike in the mountains on the weekends with Anne.

No, I can't. I don't date her anymore. What do you and your wife do for exercise?

SHOES
SALE

I play golf twice a month. My wife likes her aerobics class. Exercise is a great habit. Hey, where are you going?

All this talk about exercise makes me tired. I'm taking a break.

OPEN AN ACCOUNT
SAVE 10% TODAY!

CHARGE

EMPLOYEE ONLY

Questions

What is Henri's problem? What does
Mark think Henri should do?
Why does Henri take a break?
How do you think Henri really feels
about exercise?

Do you like to exercise? Why?
Which of Mark's ideas for exercise do
you like best?

50

Vocabulary

Look at the words and pictures. Listen to your teacher. Say the words.

exercise = normal physical activity
twice = two times

habit = something you usually do
to lose weight = to weigh less

Ways to Exercise

| aerobics | karate | to hike in the mountains | to lift weights | to play golf | to ride a bicycle | to swim |

Your Words

_____

_____

Exercise 1 Mark does many kinds of exercises. Look at the exercise activities above. Which activities can you do outdoors? Which activities can you do indoors? Which activities can you do both indoors and outdoors? Write the activities in the chart below. Add your own ideas.

Outdoor Activities	Indoor Activities	Indoor and Outdoor Activities
play golf		

Listening

Exercise 2 Henri has to decide what kind of exercise he will do. In a survey, a radio station asks people about their exercise habits. Listen to the information. Complete the chart.

Caller	Age	Kind of Exercise	How Often
Caller 1	33	_____	_____
Caller 2	48	_____	_____
Caller 3	67	_____	_____
Caller 4	22	_____	_____
Caller 5	51	_____	_____

After You Listen Compare answers with a partner.

Your Turn

With a partner, ask and answer these questions about exercise. What kind of exercise do you do? Do you like to exercise indoors or outdoors? How often do you exercise?

SPOTLIGHT on Review Subject and Object Pronouns

<u>I</u> take **aerobics classes.** <u>They</u> help **me** lose weight.
subject   object   subject   object

<u>You</u> lift **weights.** <u>The trainer</u> helps **you.**

<u>Mark</u> takes a **karate class.** <u>He</u> takes **it** once a week.

<u>Ms. Yamashita</u> helps **Mark.** <u>She</u> helps **him.**

<u>Mark</u> is teaching **his wife** to play golf. <u>He</u> teaches **her** once a week.

<u>The karate teachers</u> help **Mark and me.** <u>They</u> help **us.**

<u>Mark and I</u> love **karate classes.** <u>We</u> want to take **them** every day.

Exercise 3 Mark decided to take a karate class. Complete the sentences. Write the correct word on the line. Use <u>me</u>, <u>you</u>, <u>him</u>, <u>her</u>, <u>it</u>, <u>us</u>, and <u>them</u>.

People exercise for many reasons. Lynn exercises to lose weight. She rides her bicycle. She rides **(1)** _____it_____ around the neighborhood. Mark has problems sleeping. Exercise helps **(2)** _____ to sleep better. Sharon exercises for her health. She takes aerobics classes at the YMCA. She takes **(3)** _____ three days a week. Victor takes karate classes to relax. He has his brown belt in karate. He earned **(4)** _____ last month. Henri wants to lose weight. He bought some weights. He lifts **(5)** _____ every day. Doctors know that exercise is important for us. They want **(6)** _____ to exercise 20 minutes at least three times a week.

Exercise 4 In your notebook, write sentences about how you exercise. Use the words on page 51 for ideas. For example, write "I like to swim. I do it once a month." "I take aerobics classes. I take them three times a week." "I sometimes play basketball."

Pair Work

Listen to the conversation between Henri and Mark. Then practice it with a partner.

Henri: Do you exercise a lot?

Mark: I sure do. I lift weights on the weekends. Do you like to exercise?

Henri: Not really. I never liked exercise. I need to find exercise I can enjoy.

Mark: You should go to the gym with us on Saturday.

Talk About It

In a group, ask and answer questions about things you do to exercise. Use the sentences in Exercise 4 to help you. For example, say "I take aerobic classes every week. They help me lose weight."

Reading for Real

Henri wants to stay healthy. He read a questionnaire about risk factors for heart disease. Risk factors are things that help cause heart disease. For example, smokers have heart disease more often than non-smokers do. Stress is also a risk factor.

Survey of Risk Factors for Heart Disease

Do you have risk factors for heart disease? If you do, you need to learn how to stay healthy.

Which risk factors for heart disease do you have? Circle yes or no.

Heart disease risk factors you can't change:

Age: Are you a man over 40 or a woman over 60?	Yes	No
Family History: Do people in your family have heart disease?	Yes	No

Heart disease risk factors you can change:

Cholesterol: Do you have high cholesterol?	Yes	No
Body fat: Are you 20 percent over your healthy weight?	Yes	No
Smoking: Do you smoke?	Yes	No
Diet: Do you eat foods high in fat, sugar, and salt?	Yes	No
Stress: Do you have a lot of stress?	Yes	No
Exercise: Do you exercise less than 20 minutes three times a week?	Yes	No

Exercise 5 Henri filled out the survey. Read the questions below. Look for the answers in the survey above. Circle the letter of the best answer.

1. Which risk factor can't you change?
   a. age
   b. cholesterol
   c. smoking

2. Which risk factor can you change?
   a. age
   b. family history
   c. exercise

3. Which group often has heart disease at a younger age?
   a. men
   b. women
   c. both groups are the same

4. What are people 20 percent over their perfect weight at risk for?
   a. heart disease
   b. smoking
   c. stress

5. How much should you exercise per week?
   a. 30 minutes five times a week
   b. 20 minutes three times a week
   c. 50 minutes five times a week

6. Who is most at risk for heart disease?
   a. 45-year-old male smoker
   b. 45-year-old female non-smoker
   c. 20-year-old man who doesn't exercise

Talk About It

In a group, ask and answer these questions about the risk factors for heart disease.
What risks do you have for heart disease?
What can you do about your risk factors?
What is difficult for you to change?

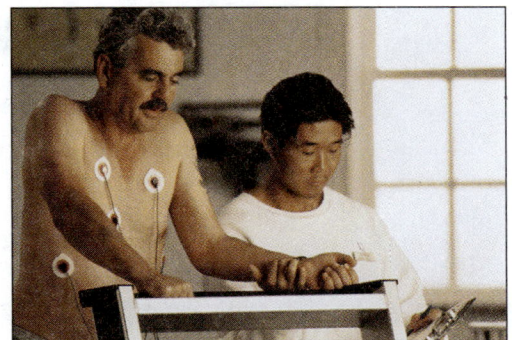

With a partner, talk about the pictures. Listen to the conversation.
Ask and answer the questions.

> **Dr. Harrison told me to order some health supplements. I'm tired a lot of the time. I don't have any energy. I want to quit smoking too.**

> **How many supplements are you going to order?**

> **I need a few bottles of herbal supplements. I'm also going to order bottles of vitamins and protein powder.**

> **OK, let me add up the cost. Wow! It's $89.55 for everything. That's a lot of money!**

Vitamin C!
1000mg tablets
BUY ONE, AND GET A SECOND FOR 50% OFF
LIMITED TIME ONLY!

Protein Powder

Calcium
AND VITAMIN D

to add up
to find the total

SUPPLEMENTS BY MAIL order form

ITEM	PRICE	QTY.	TOTAL
Vitamin E 400 mg	6.98	2	13.96
St. John's Wort	9.15	1	9.15
Protein Powder	17.98	2	35.96
Vitamin C 1000mg SALE	15.00	2	22.50
Selenium	7.98	1	7.98
		TOTAL	$ 89.55

Freshness guaranteed!
Shipped in 24

Questions

What is Mark's health problem?
What is Mark going to order from the catalog?
Why is Mark surprised about the price?
Why do you think Mark wants to quit smoking?

Do you buy health supplements?
Are health supplements expensive?

Vocabulary

Look at the words. Listen to your teacher. Say the words.

    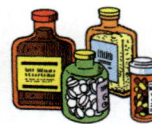 

capsule   **herbal =** made from plants   **powder**   **protein**   **supplement =** something that adds protein or vitamins to the body   **to quit (smoking) =** to stop (smoking)

energy = the ability to do things; strength
vitamins = a part of food, sometimes named A, B, or C.
to change (one's) mind = to make a different decision

Exercise 6 Mark told Sharon that he wants to order supplements. Complete the sentences. Use the words above to help you. Write the correct word on the line.

1. _____Vitamins_____ in food, such as A, B, C, and D, are needed for good health.

2. _____ in food helps your body to be strong and healthy. It is in meat and eggs.

3. A _____ is something that is added to your diet for good health.

4. _____ supplements come from plants. Some people believe they can be good for your health.

5. You have lots of _____. You do not get tired quickly.

6. A _____ is a kind of pill.

Listening

Exercise 7 Listen to Mark talking to his wife about the health supplements catalog order form. Fill in the information in the chart below.

After You Listen

Compare your answers with a partner.

Talk About It

In a group, add up Mark's order, including shipping. Check your answers with another group. What did Mark decide not to buy? Do you think supplements are good for him? Why or why not? Do you need supplements?

Order Form for ABC Health Supplements

Quantity	Item	Cost per item	Total cost for items
1 can	_____	$ 17.98	$17.98
_____	ABC Vitamin E	$ 6.98	_____
1 bottle	_____	$ 15.00	$15.00
_____	St. John's Wort	$ 9.15	_____
		Subtotal	_____
		Shipping (10%)	_____
		TOTAL	_____

SPOTLIGHT on Future with Be + Going To

Affirmative

I am (I'm) going to buy supplements next week.

You are (You're) going eat protein today.

Sharon is (Sharon's) going to buy vitamins.

We are (We're) going to eat fruit today today.

Mark and Sharon are going to exercise later.

Negative

I'm not going to buy supplements next week.

You aren't (You're not) going to eat protein today.

She isn't (She's not) going to buy vitamins.

We aren't (We're not) going to eat fruit

They aren't (They're not) going to exercise later.

Question

Are you going to exercise tonight?

No, I'm not going to exercise tonight.

Exercise 8 Mark and Sharon are going to exercise and stay healthy. Complete the sentences. Write the correct word on the line. Use the future with <u>be going to</u>.

1. Mark _____ is going to _____ buy some supplements next week.

2. Sharon _____ get more exercise.

3. He _____ lift weights.

4. They **(not)** _____ exercise on Saturday.

5. _____ you _____ lower your risk of heart disease by eating healthier?

6. You **(not)** _____ be healthier if you don't eat protein.

7. He **(not)** _____ go to the gym tonight.

8. We _____ quit smoking.

Exercise 9 What are you going to do next week to be healthier? In your notebook, write three sentences using <u>be going to</u> + verb. You can write about food, exercise, or sleep. For example, write "I'm going to drink six glasses of water every day."

Talk About It

In a group, talk about healthy things you're going to do. The first student tells the group one healthy thing he or she is going to do. The next student reports the information, then tells the group something he or she is going to do.

For example:

Mark: I'm going to sleep more.

Sharon: Mark is going to sleep more. I'm going to take aerobics classes. What are you going to do, Henri?

Henri: Mark is going to sleep more. Sharon is going to take aerobics classes. I'm going to lift weights.

SPOTLIGHT on Count and Noncount Nouns

Count Nouns

How many hours do you sleep?
  I sleep **many** hours every night.
  I sleep **a few** hours every night.
How many bottles do you have?
  We have **some** bottles.
  We don't have **many (a lot of)** bottles.
  We don't have **any** bottles.

Noncount Nouns

How much exercise does Sharon get?
  She gets **a lot** of exercise.
  She gets **a little** exercise.
How much water do you think?
  I drink **some** water.
  I don't drink **much (a lot of)** water.
  I don't drink **any** water.

Count nouns are separate things you can count.
They have both a singular and a plural form: one hour, two hours; one bottle, three bottles.
Use **some, a lot of/many** and **a few** with count nouns in affirmative statements.
Use **any, a lot of/many** with count nouns in negative statements.

Noncount nouns are complete things. You cannot count them separately.
You have to measure them.
Incorrect: a sugar, a water   Correct: a box of sugar, a bottle of water

Use **some, a lot of** and **a little** with noncount nouns in affirmative statements.
Use **any, a lot of/much** with noncount nouns in negative statements.

Use **some** or **any** in yes/no questions with both count and noncount nouns.
Do you get **any** exercise?   Yes, I get **some** exercise every day.
Do you have **some** vitamins?   No, I don't have **any** vitamins.

Exercise 10 Before starting new exercise, Sharon talked to her doctor. Complete the sentences. Write the correct word on the line. Use <u>many</u>, <u>much</u>, <u>a lot of</u>, <u>some</u>, <u>a few</u>, <u>a little</u>, and <u>any</u>.

Doctor: How **(1)** _____ much _____ exercise do you get?

Sharon: I get **(2)** _____ exercise. I walk two times a week.

Doctor: How **(3)** _____ sleep do you get every night?

Sharon: I get **(4)** _____ sleep. Usually I get five or six hours.

Doctor: How **(5)** _____ supplements do you take each day?

Sharon: I take **(6)** _____ supplements every day.

Pair Work

Listen to the conversation between Mark and Sharon. Then practice it with a partner.

Mark: I am going to buy a lot of vitamins today.
Sharon: That's good. Are you going to get any exercise today?
Mark: Yes, after dinner tonight. Are you going to take a nap later?
Sharon: Yes, I'll sleep for a few hours this afternoon.

Your Turn

With a partner, ask and answer the doctor's questions from Exercise 9. Then, change roles and ask the questions again.

Organizing Your Ideas

Henri finally decided to exercise because he knows it is good for him. Think about the reasons exercise is good for you. Write your reasons in the circles below.

Lose weight

Reasons to Exercise

Now think about ways you like to exercise. Write your favorites in the circles below.

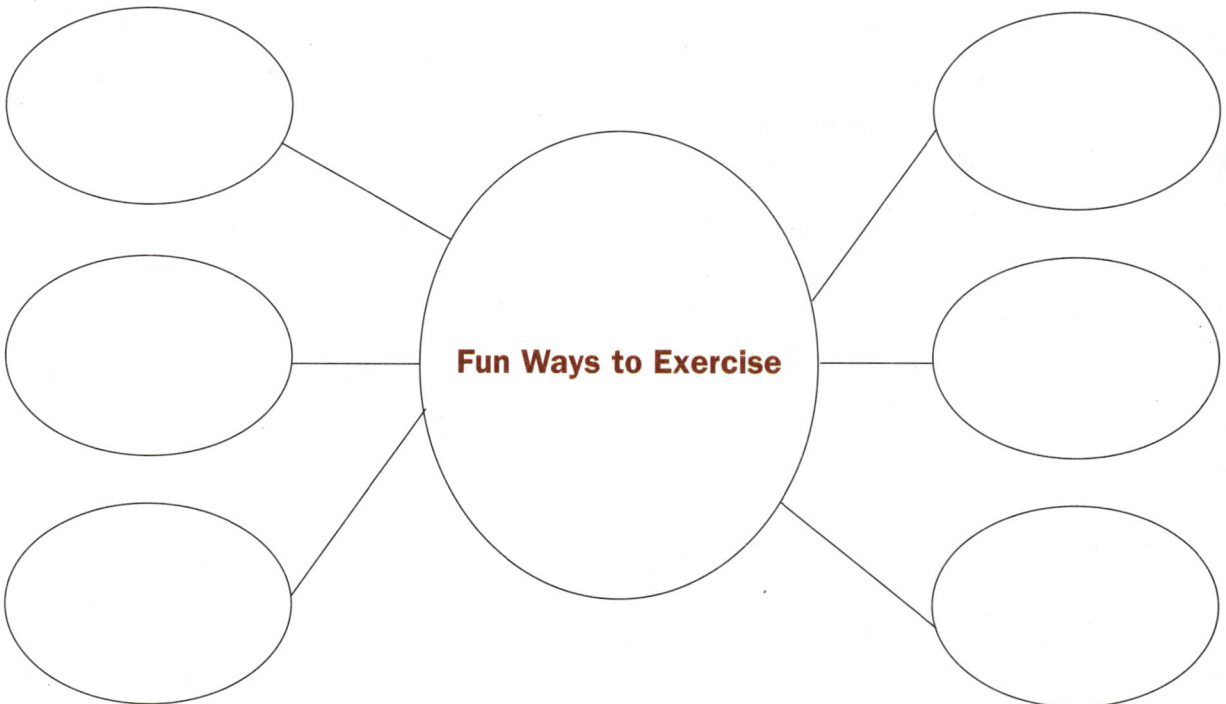

Fun Ways to Exercise

Talk About It

In a group, talk about the ways you exercise and why these ways are good for you. Ask and answer these questions. What is the best way to exercise? Why?

Issues and Answers

Big Bob wants to lose weight. Read the letter and Dr. Brownlee's advice. Then talk with other students about the advice. Do you agree? What other advice can you give?

Ask Dr. Brownlee

DEAR DR. BROWNLEE,

I have a problem. I need to lose weight. I know I have risk factors for heart disease. It's hard for me to eat healthy foods. I know exercise can help me. But I don't like to exercise very much. Can you tell me some easy and fun ways to exercise?

—BIG BOB

DEAR BIG BOB,

You're right! Exercise can help you with your weight. You need to find the best exercise for you. You're going to have fun with the right exercise. Everyone likes different ways to exercise. Find two or three ways to exercise that you like. Exercise four or five times a week for at least 20 minutes. Make a plan and stay with it. Good luck with your goal.

—DR. BROWNLEE

Your Turn

Big Bob is going to exercise to lose weight. Do you have an exercise plan?

Step 1: With a partner, list the ways you both like to exercise. Use your idea maps on page 58.

Step 2: Plan an exercise schedule for one week for you and your partner. Include two or three different ways to exercise. Make a schedule. Both partners should agree on what to do, and when, where, and how many minutes they should exercise.

Step 3: Share your ideas with the class. Who has the best schedule? Why?

Community Involvement

Medical care is expensive. Workers often have heath insurance to pay for health screenings. But what happens to people with no health insurance? Some places in the United States give health screenings for little or no cost.

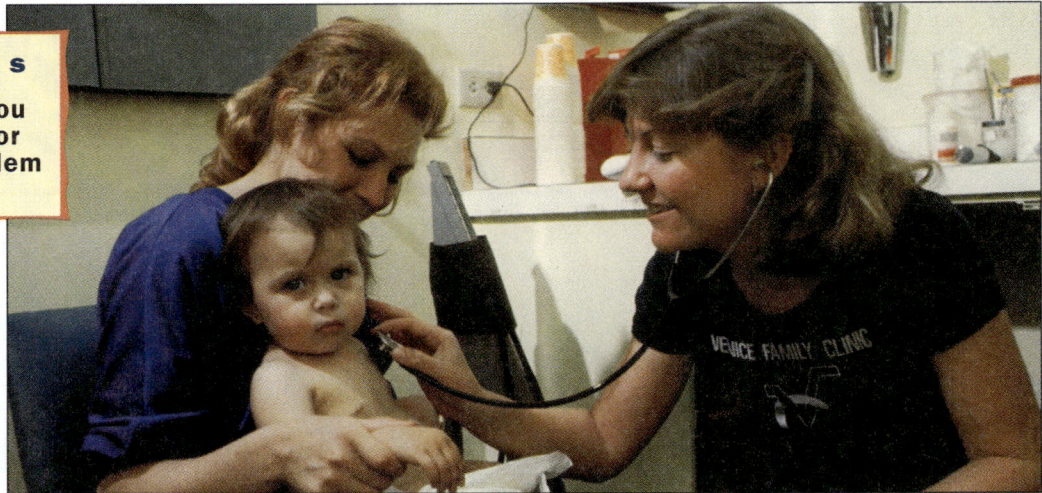

screenings

tests to see if you have a disease or other health problem

Your Turn

With a partner, talk about health screenings. Were free health screenings available in your native country? Do you know any clinics or other places in your U.S. neighborhood that offer free health screenings? What are the screenings for?

Community Action

Step 1: With a partner, find information about inexpensive or free health screenings in your community. Ask an English speaker, look in the telephone book, or do an Internet search for "free health screenings" and the name of your city or town. Where are the free health screenings in your community? Below, write the name, address, and phone number of the low-cost screening service that's near your home.

· Clinic or Medical Office Name _____
· Address _____
· Telephone number _____

Step 2: Call the service you found in Step 1, or go to its web site on the Internet. Find the answers to these questions and write them in your notebook.
· What health screenings does the service offer?
· Are there services to help people lose weight, stop drinking, or quit smoking?
· Who can use this service? When is the health service open?
· Are there any fees for the service? If so, how much?

Talk About It

In a group, talk about the information you learned about free health screenings. What screenings are available in your neighborhood? Make a chart for the class of this information. Include name, address, phone number, services, hours, and who can use the services.

Wrap Up

Mark, Sharon and Henri found ways to be healthy. How do you stay healthy? Fill in the circles below. Write different ways you can be healthy.

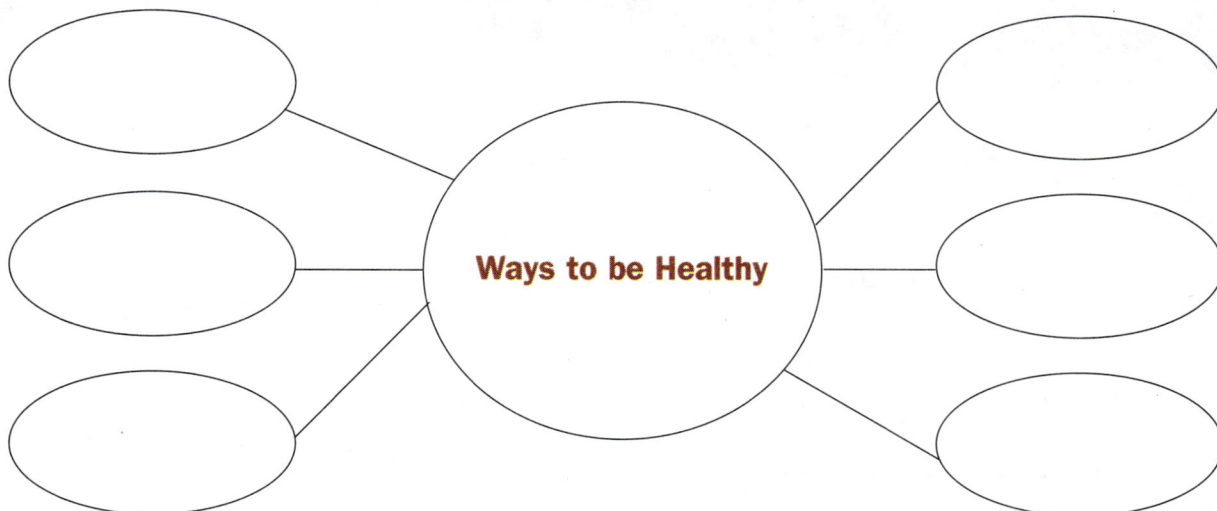

(idea map diagram with center circle labeled "Ways to be Healthy" connected to six empty ovals)

With a partner, role-play a conversation at a clinic. One person is the doctor. One person is the patient. Use words from the unit, object pronouns, future with **be going to,** and count and noncount nouns. For example:

A: There are many risk factors for heart disease. Let's see if you have any of them. Do you exercise often?

B: Oh, yes. I exercise every day.

A: Do you smoke?

B: Yes, I smoke a few cigarettes on weekends.

A: You need to quit smoking if you are going to be healthy.

Practice your role-play. Then share it with the class.

Think About Learning

Check (✔) to show your learning in this unit. Then write one more thing you learned.

SKILLS / STRUCTURES	PAGE	EASY ☺	SO-SO 😐	DIFFICULT ☹
Talk about exercise and healthy habits	50, 54			
Understand conversations about exercise and health supplements	51, 55			
Use subject and direct object pronouns	52			
Read information about health risks	53			
Use future with **be going to**	56			
Use count and noncount nouns	57			
Create an idea map to organize your ideas	58			
Write a schedule	59			
Learn about low cost health screenings in your community	60			

Scene 1: Conversation

**With a partner, talk about the pictures. Listen to the conversation.
Ask and answer the questions.**

Mei is talking to her friend Nicole.

*I want to work at home.
I need a desk, chair, and lamp for my
home office. Nicole, where can I find
some bargains? Most stores are
expensive.*

*There are many places that
cost less money. Discount stores
and flea markets are cheaper than
regular stores. Factory outlets
have good deals too.*

50 STORES
FACTORY OUTLET
SAVE-A-LOT DISCOUNT
FLEA MARKET SATURDAY
FURNITURE SALE

*What is the
least expensive
place?*

*The cheapest place
is probably a yard sale. It's
harder to find good furniture,
but the prices are great! There was
a yard sale in my neighborhood
last weekend.*

TOYS
$5
$1

Questions

What does Mei need to buy? Why?

What is the problem with regular stores?

Which places does Nicole tell Mei about?

Which place is the cheapest?

Where do you go to find a bargain?

Which place do you think has the best prices?

Vocabulary

Look at the words. Listen to your teacher. Say the words.

| discount store | factory outlet | flea market | secondhand store | classified ads | yard sale |

bargain = lower than the usual price
cheap = not expensive
used = owned by someone else before
to prefer = to like one thing more than another
to hunt = to look for

Your Words

_____

_____

Exercise 1 Mei decided to look at different stores for the things she wants to buy. Match the definitions in Column B to the words in Column A. Write the letter.

COLUMN A

1. ___e___ discount store
2. _____ secondhand store
3. _____ factory outlet
4. _____ classified ads
5. _____ flea market
6. _____ yard sale
7. _____ bargain
8. _____ cheap

COLUMN B

a. not expensive
b. information about used items for sale in the newspaper
c. store that sells things from the factory at a lower cost
d. people sell their used items in their garage or yard
e. store that sells new things at a lower cost than other stores
f. a good price, lower than usual
g. store that sells used things
h. place where many different people sell their used items

Listening

Exercise 2 Listen to Mei's friends describing the places they shop. Check (✔) the things each store has or does.

	New products	Used products	Good prices	Best prices	Store delivers
Secondhand store					
Yard sale					
Factory outlet					
Classified ads					
Flea market					

After You Listen Compare your answers with a partner.

Your Turn

With a partner, talk about the different stores in Exercise 2. Which places do you prefer? Why?

SPOTLIGHT on Comparative Adjectives

Her lamp is small. My lamp is **smaller.**
The brown desk is big. The black desk is **bigger.**
The flea market is **busier** today than it was yesterday.
That chair is **more comfortable** than our chair.
Their computer is **more expensive** than ours.
My computer is **less powerful** than Jack's.

$$ less expensive $$$$ more expensive

To compare animals, things, or people, add **-er** to adjectives with one syllable.
For most adjectives with two or more syllables, use **more** or **less** before the adjective.
For two-syllable adjectives ending in **-y**, change **-y** to **i** and add **-er.**
Use **than** after every comparative adjective.

big—**bigger**	good—**better**	expensive—**more expensive**
bad—**worse**	busy—**busier**	

For a list of common comparative adjectives, see page 122.

> **rebate**
>
> money a store or company gives back to lower the price of something

Exercise 3 Mei and Nicole are shopping for chairs and lamps at a discount store. Replace the adjectives below with comparative adjectives.

Mei: I think I'll buy this black chair. It's a **(1) good** _____*better*_____ bargain than the others.

Nicole: But how about that blue chair? It's **(2) large** _____, and it looks **(3) comfortable** _____ than the black chair.

Mei: I prefer the **(4) small** _____ chair because my room is very small. And the black chair is **(5) cheap** _____, too. That's important. Now let's look at lamps.

Nicole: This white lamp is **(6) expensive** _____ than that red one, but it has a $10.00 rebate. It's also **(7) pretty** _____ and **(8) big** _____ than the red lamp.

Exercise 4 In your notebook, write two sentences comparing two different things in the classroom. For example, write "The students' chairs are smaller and less comfortable than the teacher's chair." "The teacher's chair is bigger and more comfortable than the students' chairs."

Pair Work

Listen to the conversation between Gabe and Mei. Then practice it with a partner.

Gabe: Did you find a good bargain at the discount store?
Mei: I bought a lamp. It had a 10 dollar rebate.
Gabe: Was the discount store cheaper than the other stores?
Mei: It sure was! The furniture was a lot less expensive.

Talk About It

In a group, use comparative adjectives to describe things in your class. Use the sentences in Exercise 4 to help you. For example, say, "Which chair do you prefer?" "I like the teacher's chair better than the student's chair. It looks more comfortable."

Reading for Real

Mei needs to buy a desk for her home office. She wants to get a bargain. In the newspaper, there are two ads for desks. One of the desks has no payments for two months. She doesn't have to pay until later. The other desk is less money. Which is the better buy for Mei?

Smull's Furniture Special	Shop at Sav-Mart
Computer Desk	Office Desk
Sale for 3 days only	$99.99
Desks for computer use	46" x 29" x 24"
Reg. $350 Sale $199	*Everyday Low Low Price*
No payments for 2 months	Join the Sav-Mart Club and save 2%.

Exercise 5 Mei can't decide which desk to buy. Read the questions below. Look for the answers in the ads above. Circle the letter of the best answer.

1. Which desk is less expensive?
   a. the computer desk
   b. the office desk
   c. both are the same price

2. Which desk can she pay for later?
   a. the computer desk
   b. the office desk
   c. both

3. What is the regular price of the computer desk?
   a. $199
   b. $350
   c. $ 99

4. What is the sale price of the computer desk?
   a. $199
   b. $350
   c. $ 99

5. How can she save with the office desk?
   a. join the Sav-Mart Club
   b. buy in three days
   c. buy now at a special low price

6. Which store is having a sale?
   a. Smull's Furniture
   b. Sav-Mart
   c. both

Talk About It

In a group, ask and answer these questions.
Which desk is a better buy for Mei? Why?
Share your answer with the class.

Scene 2: Conversation

With a partner, talk about the pictures. Listen to the conversation. Ask and answer the questions.

Mei wants to find a bargain computer. She is asking Nicole for help.

I need a computer, but the computers at Compquick are too expensive. Do you know of any bargains?

How about a used computer? I saw used computers at Al's Computers last week. He has the best prices in town!

I can buy the latest model with a credit card. I have an application right here. Don't worry. I will pay the entire balance in three months.

Well, be careful. I had a credit card last year. There were lots of fees. I used my credit card too much. I paid a lot of money in interest, late fees and over limit fees.

Questions

Why doesn't Mei want to buy her computer at Compquick?

What is Nicole's idea about computers?

How is Mei going to buy the computer?

What were Nicole's problems with a credit card?

Do you have a credit card? Do you like it?

Do you know people with credit card problems?

Vocabulary

Look at the words. Listen to your teacher. Say the words.

to charge something = to use a credit card to buy something
balance = total amount of money you need to pay on your credit card
interest = extra money you pay for having a credit card balance
late fee = extra money you pay for paying a bill late
limit = the largest amount of money you can charge on your credit card
model = one kind of machine or product
over limit fee = extra money you pay for charging more than the limit on a credit card

Exercise 6 Mei and Nicole talked about credit cards. Complete the sentences. Use the words above to help you. Write the correct word on the line.

1. Mei wants a new XT 3I computer. She only wants that _____model_____, not any other computer.

2. Nicole has a _____ of $5000 on her credit card. She can't charge more than that.

3. Nicole didn't pay all of her credit card balance last month. She has to pay _____.

4. Nicole must pay an _____ if she charges more than her limit.

5. Nicole paid her bill late one month. She had to pay a _____ of $29.00.

6. Mei is going _____ the computer on her credit card.

Listening

Exercise 7 Mei is going to complete a credit card application. She is asking Nicole for help. Listen to their conversation. Write the correct information on the line.

Credit Card Application	**applicant**
	person who applies

Applicant Information (Please print in black or blue ink.)

Applicant (full name) _____Mei Ling_____

Birthdate _____ Social Security Number ___316-88-1234___

Yearly Income _____ Home Phone ___(316) 555-4622___

Employer: ___Jay's Market___ Employer's Phone: _____

Position: ___Cashier___

Residence: ☐ Own   ☐ Rent   Monthly Housing Payment $_____

Mother's Maiden Name ___Tan___

E-mail Address _____

Applicant Signature ___Mei Ling___   Date ___March 27, 2003___

The _____ is $29.00. The _____ is $35.00

After You Listen Compare your answers with a partner.

Your Turn

With a partner, look at the application in Exercise 7 again. Ask and answer questions about Mei's application. For example, say "What is Mei's birthdate?" Share your answers with the class.

SPOTLIGHT on Superlative Adjectives

This is **the smallest** lamp in the store.
The brown desk is **the biggest** one in the store.
That is **the best** chair in the store.
This is **the busiest** computer store in the city.
This is **the least expensive** computer in the store.
That computer is **the most powerful** one in the store.

To make superlative adjectives, add **-est** to one-syllable adjectives.
For two-syllable adjectives ending in **-y**, change the **-y** to **i** and add **-est.**

For other adjectives with two or more syllables, use **most** or **least** before the adjective.
Use **the** before all superlative adjectives.

big—**the biggest**	good—**the best**	bad—**the worst**
busy—**the busiest**	expensive—**the least expensive**	
	powerful—**the most powerful**	

For a list of common superlative adjectives, see page 122.

---

booth

a place at a market where you can buy things

Exercise 8 Mei's friends Gabe and Rosa are at a flea market shopping for things for their home. Use superlative adjectives to complete the sentences.

Gabe: Rosa, let's go to the flea market on Adams Avenue this weekend. It is

(1) big _____*the biggest*_____ flea market in town. Also, it's (2) close

_____ one to us.

Rosa: All right. I don't have much money, so I need to buy (3) expensive

_____ lamp in the place.

Gabe: Look at that booth! There are 50 people there! It's (4) busy

_____ booth at the whole flea market.

Rosa: Look over there! That is (5) large _____ and (6) beautiful

_____ desk here.

Gabe: Let's go to that booth. It has (9) low _____ prices and (10) good

_____ choices in the flea market.

Exercise 9 In your notebook, write about your favorite places to shop and why. What is your favorite supermarket? discount store? clothing store? secondhand store? For example, write "I shop at Smith's Food Market. They have the best prices for fruit."

Talk About It

In a group, talk about where you can find the best bargains. Use the sentences in Exercise 9 to help you. For example, ask "What do you think is the best discount store? I like Sav-Mart because they have the lowest prices on tools."

SPOTLIGHT on Too + Adjectives and Quantifiers

The computer is **too expensive**. I can't buy it.

The clerk was **too busy**. She couldn't help me.

The sweaters were **too small**. We couldn't wear them.

The desk is **too heavy**. They can't carry it to their car.

You bought **too many** gifts. You'll have to return some of them.

She charged **too much** on her credit card. Now she has to pay over limit fees.

Too + adjective and **too much** or **too many** mean more than you want or need.

Exercise 10 Mei has to decide which computer to buy. Complete the sentences. Write the correct words on the lines. Use <u>too</u> and the words below.

old	expensive	small	difficult	much	many

Mei is looking for a computer. She saw one in a discount store for $1200, but that was

(1) ___*too expensive*___ for her. She saw a used computer in a flea market for $200,

but it was five years old. That was (2) _____ for her. Now Mei is

thinking about using a credit card to buy the computer, but she's worried. She knows

some people spend (3) _____ money with credit cards. Some of Mei's

friends have seven or eight credit cards. Mei thinks that's (4) _____

cards. She only wants one card. Spending a lot of money on credit cards can make it

(5) _____ to pay the credit card bill every month.

Exercise 11 In your notebook, write three sentences about you. Use <u>too</u> + adjective and <u>too much</u> or <u>too many</u>. For example, write, " I want a computer, but I can't buy one. They're too expensive and have too many problems."

Pair Work

Listen to the conversation between Nicole and Mei. Then practice it with a partner.

Nicole: Did you buy your new computer yesterday?
Mei: No, the one I wanted was too expensive.
Nicole: Are you going to shop at the factory outlet this weekend?
Mei: It's too far away. I'll have to find a closer store with better prices.

Talk About It

In a group, talk about something you wanted to do or buy, but you didn't. Explain the reason. Use **too** + adjective. For example, say "I wanted to buy a big table with eight chairs, but my apartment is too small. I bought a small table with four chairs."

Organizing Your Ideas

Mei wants to buy furniture and a computer for her home office. She needs to know reasons she should or shouldn't buy used things. What are your reasons to buy or not to buy something used? Write your reasons in the chart below. Use the words on pages 63 and 67 to help you.

Reasons to Buy Used Things	Reasons NOT to Buy Used Things
Used things are cheaper than new things.	Used things are often dirtier than new things.

debt

money you have to pay for past and present bills

Mei is thinking about getting a credit card to buy the computer she wants. Help her decide what to do. Place these reasons to have a credit card or not to have a credit card in the chart below. Think of two more reasons and write them in the chart.

Maybe you will buy more things than you need.
You can pay the bill later.
Maybe you will have problems with debt.
You can buy something in an emergency.

You can buy something better.
You don't have to carry money with you.
Maybe you will pay extra fees.
Maybe you will pay a higher price because of the interest.

Reasons to Have a Credit Card	Reasons NOT to Have a Credit Card

Talk About It

In a group, talk about your charts. Is it better for Mei to buy new or used things? What do you think is the biggest problem with a credit card? What is the best reason to have a credit card? Is it better for Mei to use a credit card or not to use a credit card? Share your ideas with the class.

Issues and Answers

Mei wrote to Ms. Moneybags for advice. Read the letter and Ms. Moneybags' advice. Then talk with other students about the advice. Do you agree? What other advice can you give?

Ask Ms. Moneybags

DEAR MS. MONEYBAGS,

I'm starting a home office. There are many expenses. Some of the things I need are too expensive for me to buy. I've shopped at discount and secondhand stores. I bought things at the flea market. But I still need to buy a fax machine. I'm thinking about getting a credit card to help me buy everything I need. My friend says that's a bad idea. She says there are too many problems with credit cards. What is your opinion of using a credit card?

—TOO LITTLE MONEY

DEAR TOO LITTLE MONEY,

Credit cards are useful. You can buy things you want or need right away, but you need to be smart with credit cards. You need to pay the bills on time or you will pay a late fee. Also, if you don't pay your monthly balance, you pay interest. There are some cards with very high APR, the yearly interest rate. Try to save for purchases first. Too much debt can be a big problem.

—MS. MONEYBAGS

> **APR**
> Annual Percentage Rate: amount of interest you pay each year

Your Turn

What other advice can you give to Too Little Money?

Step 1: With a partner, look at your charts on page 70. Which do you think will be the better bargain, a less expensive fax machine bought with a credit card, or a more expensive fax machine bought on sale with cash.

Step 2: Figure out the cost of buying a $200 fax machine from TRON on a credit card. The credit card has a 15% APR. Figure out the cost of interest at 15% and add to the price. This is the price of the machine if you pay the balance after one year. Next, figure out the cost of buying a VEGA fax machine with cash. This machine is usually $260, but is now on sale for 15% off the regular price. What is the sale price of the VEGA?

Step 3: Now compare the costs of the two fax machines. What is the difference in price of the machines? Is it cheaper for her to buy the TRON fax machine with a credit card, or the VEGA fax machine on sale with cash? Did you make the right choice in Step 1? Share your answer with the class.

Community Involvement

Do you want to save money? Look for coupons in newspapers and magazines, and use them to save money on things you buy. You can use them for drinks, pizza, frozen foods, office supplies, and other things. You can often save 10% to 20% off the price. Many people save a lot of money every year with coupons. But be careful. Sometimes people buy things they don't really need because they have coupons. Some things you buy with coupons are more expensive than other things without coupons.

Your Turn

With a partner, talk about coupons. How can coupons help you? Do you use coupons? Did you use coupons in your native country? What did you buy with coupons?

Community Action

Step 1: Find coupons from different places in your community. You can find them in the newspaper, in magazines, in stores, in your mailbox, and in flyers at your door. Bring some coupons to class. In your notebook, make a list of the places where you found the coupons.

Step 2: In a group, share your coupons. Find the answers to these questions.

Where did you find the coupons? _____

What things or services are the coupons for? _____

How much can you save with each coupon? _____

Which coupons can save you the most money? _____

Talk About It

In a group, talk about the coupons you found and your plans for them. Are you going to use any of the coupons? Which ones? Why? Share your answers with the class.

Wrap Up

Mei learned all about shopping in her town, the best places to shop, and where to find coupons to save more money. Where are the best places to shop in your neighborhood? In your notebook, make a T-chart like the one below. Write three of your favorite stores, and the reasons why you like them. Use comparative and superlative adjectives.

Favorite Store	Reason I like it
Al's Computers	most computer games in town
Smith's Supermarket	better vegetables than Tom's Grocery
Donna's Fashions	least expensive place to buy clothes

With a partner, talk about your favorite stores. Use words from this unit, and comparative and superlative adjectives. If you don't like one of your partner's stores, tell them why. Use **too** + adjective. For example:

A: My favorite computer store is Al's Computers.
B: Really? Why do you like it?
A: Al's has the best computer games in town.
B: That's true, but I think CompuQuick is a better computer store. Al's is too expensive.
A: You're right. CompuQuick is cheaper. I should shop there first.

Practice one of your conversations. Then share it with the class.

Think About Learning

Check (✔) to show your learning in this unit. Then write one more thing you learned.

SKILLS / STRUCTURES	PAGE	EASY 😊	SO-SO 😐	DIFFICULT 😟
Talk about places to shop and using credit	62,66			
Understand conversations about places to shop and using credit	63, 67			
Use comparative adjectives	64			
Read and compare sale ads	65			
Understand a credit card application	67			
Use superlative adjectives	68			
Use **too** + adjectives and qualifiers	69			
Make a chart to organize your ideas	70			
Learn about coupons in your community	72			

Scene 1: Conversation

With a partner, talk about the pictures. Listen to the conversation. Ask and answer the questions.

Alex and his wife, Julia, are looking for an apartment.
They are talking to an apartment manager.

I'm Alex Costa and this is my wife Julia. We're thinking about moving. We have too much furniture for a furnished apartment. How much is the rent for an unfurnished apartment?

Our unfurnished three-bedroom apartments are $1050 per month, with a security deposit of $1000. We're having a special of 50% off the first month's rent.

Can we look at the apartment now?

Later . . .

We really like the apartment. Do we sign a lease?

First I need you to complete this application form. I need your bank account number, current and previous addresses, information about your job, and some other information.

Rental Application

Questions

What are Alex and Julia looking for?
How much is the apartment per month?
What special is the manager offering?
What information does Alex need for the application?

Is it difficult to look for an apartment? Why?
Do you prefer a furnished or unfurnished apartment? Why?

Vocabulary

Look at the words. Listen to your teacher. Say the words.

security deposit = money you give to the landlord before you move in for any damage you cause
current address = place you live now
previous address = place you lived before
dependent = someone you take care of with food, clothes and a place to live

to own = to buy something and have it for yourself
to rent = to pay money each month for a place to live that you do not own
to move = to change the place where you live

apartment manager = person who takes care of the apartment building

furnished = with furniture

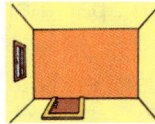

unfurnished = without furniture

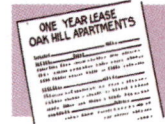

lease = a document you sign when you rent an apartment

Exercise 1 Alex and Julia want to rent an apartment. Match the words in Column A with the definitions in Column B. Write the letter.

COLUMN A	COLUMN B
1. _d_ previous address	a. people for whom you provide food, clothes, and a place to live
2. _____ current address	b. legal paper for renting a house or apartment
3. _____ security deposit	c. money you give to the apartment manager before you move in
4. _____ dependents	d. address you had before
5. _____ lease	e. address you have now

Listening

Exercise 2 Alex and Julia had to fill out a rental application. Listen to the information. Complete the form.

Application for Apartment Rental

Current address _1130 5th Avenue, Apt. 7G, Newton_   How many years? _____

Previous address _277_   _Newton_   How many years? _____

Current employer _____   How many years? _8_____

Employer's address _153_   _Newton_

Number of dependents _____

Bank account# _1183029_   Current balance _____

After You Listen Compare your answers with a partner.

Talk About It

In a group, ask and answer these questions about the application. Why does the manager ask for information about dependents and bank accounts? Do you think this is right? Why or why not? Alex is going to sign a one-year lease. What do you think happens if Alex and his family leave the apartment before one year?

Am / is / are + a verb ending in -ing show an action that is happening now.

I **am signing** a lease.
You **are giving** your landlord a security deposit.
Julia **is looking** for an apartment.
We **are looking** for an apartment.
They **are signing** a lease.
Is she **looking** for an apartment?   Yes, she **is.**

Am / is / are + a verb ending in -ing can also be used to talk about the future.

He **is looking** for an apartment next week.   We**'re looking** for an apartment next week.
Are you **looking** for an apartment tomorrow?   No, I**'m not.** I'm going to look on Tuesday.

Exercise 3 Read about Alex and Julia and the kind of apartment they want.
Complete the sentences. Write the correct words on the line. Use present progressive.

Alex and Julia **(1) look** _____are looking_____ for a three-bedroom apartment. Their

son Roberto **(2) hope** _____ to have a park nearby. Their daughter

(3) think _____ about living near her friends. Right now, the family

(4) look _____ at an apartment. Alex **(5) talk** _____

to the manager. Julia **(6) walk** _____ through the kitchen.

Exercise 4 In your notebook, write present progressive sentences about things you
are doing right now and about things you will do soon. Use words like <u>look</u>, <u>watch</u>,
<u>hope</u>, <u>talk</u>, and <u>write</u>. For example, write, "I'm writing in my notebook now. I'm
taking my father to the doctor this afternoon."

Pair Work

Listen to the conversation between the apartment manager and Alex. Then practice it
with a partner.

Manager: Are you looking for a furnished apartment?
Alex: No, I'm looking for an unfurnished apartment. We have our own furniture.
Manager: We have a nice three-bedroom unfurnished apartment.
Alex: Can we look at it now?

Talk About It

In a group, take turns asking and answering questions about what people in the group
are doing soon. Use the sentences from Exercise 4 to help you. For example, "What are
you doing tomorrow?" "I'm having lunch with my friend."

Reading for Real

Alex is still looking for a home to rent. He is reading ads in the newspaper. He sees many abbreviations in the ads. In addition to apartments, he sees there are other places to rent, such as houses, condominiums, and mobile homes.

Furnished Apartment
Near downtown, pool
2 BR, 1.5 BA, nice
furniture, $650.
Come and see!
555-1318

Condo Unfurnished
$795, 2 BR 2BA
stove, refrig. **555-0039**

House for Rent Unfurnished
$1195. Large 3 BR
2 BA, yard, garage. **555-9811**

Mobile home
$670 trailer & space, quiet.
pets OK, near shopping. Water incl.
$200 deposit. **555-4892**

Exercise 5 Alex found a lot of information about rental homes. Read the questions below. Look for the answers in the ads above. Circle the letter of the best answer.

1. What is the most expensive rental?
   a. the furnished apartment
   b. the unfurnished condo
   c. the house

2. What is the least expensive rental?
   a. the furnished apartment
   b. the unfurnished condo
   c. the mobile home

3. Which rental allows pets?
   a. the furnished apartment
   b. the unfurnished condo
   c. the mobile home

4. What information is included in all four ads?
   a. the rent
   b. the location
   c. the number of bedrooms

5. What information is not included in all four rental ads?
   a. the telephone number
   b. a pool
   c. the price

6. What information is not included in the House for Rent ad?
   a. the price
   b. the location
   c. the yard

Talk About It

In a group, ask and answer these questions.
Why do some people like furnished rentals more than unfurnished rentals? Which of the four rentals do you like? Why?

With a partner, talk about the pictures. Listen to the conversation. Ask and answer the questions.

Alex and Julia were going to rent an apartment.
Now they are thinking about buying a house.

Are you sure you want to buy a house? Are you sure we can afford it?

Yes, I'm sure. We earn enough money to pay a mortgage.

FOR SALE CALL

We'll have lots more responsibilities. You'll need to make repairs, and they will be expensive.

I know, but a house is an investment. We'll be saving more money than renting. We'll look for a fixer-upper. That will be cheaper. And I know we can qualify for a loan.

All right, let's do it! I'll call a real estate agent.

cell-mate

Questions

What does Alex want to do?

What are Julia's worries about a house?

Why is a house an investment?

Who will Julia call?

What are some of the responsibilities of owning a home?

Which do you think has more responsibilities—owning your own home or renting?

Vocabulary

Look at the words. Listen to your teacher. Say the words.

fixer-upper = a house that needs lots of repairs

real estate agent

to decorate

down payment = first payment to buy a home
investment = something you buy that you can sell for more money
loan = money you borrow from a bank
mortgage = a loan from a bank to buy a house or condominium

responsibilities = things you have to do
to afford = to have enough money to buy something
to qualify = to show the bank that you have enough money to pay back a loan

Exercise 6 Julia and Alex are thinking about buying a house. Complete the sentences. Use the words above to help you. Write the correct word on the line.

1. Most people get a _____loan_____ to buy a house. They have to borrow money from the bank to pay for the house.
2. People need to _____ for a loan. They need to show they have enough money to make the payments.
3. A _____ is a person who can help you buy a house.
4. The money you pay when you first buy a house is a _____.
5. A _____ is a house that needs repairs.
6. A house comes with many _____. You have to make repairs, take care of the yard, and pay taxes.

Listening

Exercise 7 Alex and Julia are still thinking about buying a house or renting an apartment. To help them decide, they wrote a list. Listen to the conversation. Write the correct information in your notebook.

Reasons to Rent an Apartment	Reasons to Buy a House
You don't have to qualify for a . . .	A house is an . . .
Renting usually costs less money a . . .	You don't have to move . . .
The manager will repair broken . . .	You can decorate a house your . . .
You don't have to take care of a . . .	You have your house for the . . .

After You Listen Compare your answers with a partner.

Talk About It

In a group, talk about Alex and Julia's ideas in Exercise 7. Do you agree or disagree with their reasons? Explain. What are other reasons to rent an apartment or to buy a house? Should Alex and Julia buy a house or rent an apartment? Share your ideas with the class.

SPOTLIGHT on Future with Will

Affirmative Statements

I **will (I'll) talk** to a real estate agent.

You **will (You'll) look at** a home.

He **will (He'll) buy** a home.

She **will (She'll) rent** an apartment.

It **will (It'll) be** a nice home.

We **will (We'll) find** an apartment

They **will (They'll) look at** a home tomorrow.

won't = will not

Negative Statements

I **won't talk** to a real estate agent.

You **won't look at** a home.

He **won't buy** a home.

She **won't rent** an apartment.

It **won't be** a nice home.

We **won't find** an apartment.

They **won't look at** a home tomorrow.

Questions

Will you **look at** a home?

Will he **talk** to a real estate agent?

Short Answers

Yes, we **will.** / No, we **won't.**

Yes, he **will.** / No, he **won't.**

Use **will** to talk about promises or plans, or to predict the future.

Exercise 8 Read about Julia and Alex. Complete the sentences. Use <u>will</u>, <u>will not</u> or <u>won't</u> and the words below. Write the correct words on the line.

go	drive	be	buy
look at	meet	show	arrive

1. Julia and Alex _____ will look _____ at houses tomorrow.

2. They _____ with Patty, the real estate agent.

3. Patty _____ many houses to Alex and Julia.

4. They _____ Patty at her office.

5. The appointment _____ at 2:00.

6. They (**not**) _____ late for the appointment.

7. They _____ in Patty's car.

8. Alex and Julia (**not**) _____ an expensive house.

Exercise 9 In your notebook, write about your future housing plans. Use future with <u>will</u>. For example, write, "I'll buy a house in a few years."

Talk About It

In a group, take turns describing your future. What will your life be like 10 years from now? For example, say, "In 10 years I'll have a better job."

SPOTLIGHT on Future Progressive

I **will (I'll) be meeting** with the real estate agent tomorrow.

You **will (You'll) be looking** for the best loan.

She **will (She'll) be waiting** at the office.

We **will (We'll) be looking** for a house at 3:00.

They **will (They'll) be finding** a mortgage for us at the bank.

I **won't be working**.

You **won't be calling** the landlord.

She **won't be eating** lunch.

We **won't be working** at 3:00.

They **won't be looking** for other loans.

Will they **be finding a mortgage for us?**   Yes, they **will.**

Will you **be working** tomorrow?   No, I **won't.**

Will be + a verb ending with **-ing** shows an action that continues over time in the future.

Exercise 10 Julia called the real estate agent. Complete the sentences. Write the correct future progressive verb on the line.

Agent: Hi. I'm Patty, and I **(1) help** ___I'll be helping___ you to find a house. **(2) look** _____ you _____ by yourself?

Julia: No, my husband **(3) go** _____ with us. But our children **(4) not come** _____ along.

Agent: I **(5) take** _____ you to different neighborhoods. I **(6) show** _____ you some new and some older homes.

Julia: **(7) See** _____ we _____ fixer-uppers?

Agent: Yes, I **(8) take** _____ you to several fixer-uppers. And I **(9) not take** _____ to any homes that are out of your budget.

Exercise 11 In your notebook, write about things you'll be doing in the near future. Use the future progressive. For example, "I'll be studying English all day tomorrow."

Pair Work

Listen to the conversation between Julia and Alex. Then practice it with a partner.

Julia: This afternoon I'll be calling banks to find a good home loan.

Alex: And I will be looking for a good fixer-upper with the agent.

Julia: The agent called and said she can't meet with you this afternoon.

Alex: Ok. I'll call her and make a new appointment for next week.

Your Turn

With a partner, talk about what you will be doing this weekend. For example, say "I will be cleaning my house all weekend. My family is coming to visit next week. They will be staying with me for two weeks."

Organizing Your Ideas

> **expenses**
>
> **things you have to pay for**

Alex and Julia have to decide if they can afford to buy a home. Make a list of expenses for renting a three-bedroom unfurnished apartment in your neighborhood. Include monthly expenses such as rent, gas and electricity. Next to each expense, write how much you think it costs in your neighborhood.

Cost of Renting an Apartment

Monthly Expenses	How Much?
Rent	
Gas and electric	
Water	

Now make a list of expenses for owning a three-bedroom house in your area. Include monthly expenses such as mortgage payments, insurance, water, gas, electricity, and yard care costs. Next to each expense, write how much you think it costs in your neighborhood.

Cost of Buying a Home

Monthly Expenses	How Much?
Mortgage	
Insurance	
Gas, electric	
Water	
Yard care costs	

Talk About It

In a group, look at your charts. Which expenses are different for buying houses and renting apartments? Which are the same? Do you think it's better to buy or rent? Why? Share your answer with the class.

Issues and Answers

Julia is still trying to decide about renting an apartment or buying a home. Read the letter and Ms. Moneybags' advice. Then talk with other students about the advice. Do you agree? What other advice can you give?

Ask Ms. Moneybags

DEAR MS. MONEYBAGS,

My husband and I are thinking about finding a new place to live. We looked at apartments, but now my husband is talking about buying a house. A house is a wonderful idea, but I'm worried. A house is expensive. I'm worried about the down payment, qualifying for a loan, and all the expenses and responsibilities. It's much easier to rent an apartment. Then we can move if we don't like it. What do you think?

—WORRIED WIFE

DEAR WORRIED WIFE,

You are right. A house is expensive and you'll have many responsibilities. In your area, a home costs an average of $180,000. But a home is a great investment for the future. You need to ask yourselves these questions: Will you be living in the same area for a long time? Can you qualify for a loan? Do you have a regular job? Do you have savings? Will you have money for other expenses? If you answer yes to all these questions, then buying a home is a good idea. Talk to a real estate agent for more information. He or she will help you with possible government assistance programs. Good luck!

—MS. MONEYBAGS

Your Turn

Help Worried Wife decide which is better: renting an apartment or buying a house?

Step 1: An apartment in Worried Wife's area rents for $900 a month. Other monthly expenses for the apartment are about $170. What is the total monthly cost of renting an apartment? House payments for owning a home in her area are usually about $1500 each month. Other monthly expenses for a house are about $340. What is the monthly cost of owning a home in her area?

Step 2: Worried Wife and her husband have an income of $2400 per month. Most people agree that monthly housing expenses should be 50% or less of monthly income. Look at your answers from Step 1. If the couple rents an apartment, what percent of their monthly income would they spend on housing? What percent would they spend each month if they buy a house?

Step 3: Look at your answers for Step 1 and Step 2. Make a decision for Worried Wife and her husband. Which is better for them—renting an apartment or buying a home? Explain your decision to the class.

Community Involvement

The government has special programs to help people pay for housing. For example, there is a rental assistance program for people who can't afford to pay rent. There is also help for people buying homes. First-time home buyers can get special help. HUD (U.S. Department of Housing and Urban Development), has federal programs. City and county offices also help families with housing costs.

Your Turn

With a partner, talk about government housing assistance programs. Are there government programs in your native country to help people buy homes? Do many people own homes in your native country? Why or why not? How do people in your native country get the money to buy homes?

Community Action

Step 1: With a partner, find information about housing assistance offices in your community. Ask an English speaker, a real estate agent, a loan officer, or look under Housing in the government information pages in the telephone book, or search on the Internet. Find the answers to these questions and write them in your notebook.

- What is the phone number and address for the housing assistance office in your city or county? (Look in the phone book in the Government pages under the title of Housing and Community Development.)
- What site on the Internet has information on HUD?
- Is there help for first-time home buyers on the HUD site? What kind?

Step 2: Find the answers to these questions. Write the answers in your notebook.

> **loan officer**
>
> bank or mortgage office employee who helps people get loans for homes

- What is the name and phone number of a real estate agent with information about government programs to help people buy homes?
- Does the agent speak your native language?
- What is the name and phone number of a loan officer in a mortgage office or bank who has information about government home loan programs?
- Does the loan officer speak your native language?

Talk About It

In a group, share the information you learned about housing assistance. Where did you find the most information: the HUD web site, the housing assistance office in your city or county, or the real estate agent or loan officer? Write important names and phone numbers in your notebook. Share your information with the class.

Wrap Up

Alex's friend, Ivan, just arrived in the United States. Alex and Julia are going to help him buy things for his unfurnished apartment. In the chart below, list some things you think he will need. Next to each item, write the amount of money you think it will cost.

Costs of an Unfurnished Apartment

Item	How Much?
Bed	$300

Next, work with a partner. Ask questions about your partner's chart. For example:

A: How much is he going to pay for a bed?

B: He'll pay about $300 for a new bed.

A: How much will it cost to buy a refrigerator?

B: He is planning to buy a used refrigerator for about $200 next week.

Who has the least expensive choices? Share that information with the class.

Think About Learning

Check (✔) to show your learning in this unit. Then write one more thing you learned.

SKILLS / STRUCTURES	PAGE	EASY 😊	SO-SO 😐	DIFFICULT 😟
Talk about different kinds of housing	74, 78			
Understand a rental application	75			
Use present progressive	76			
Read housing ads	77			
Compare reasons to rent or buy	79, 83			
Use future with **will**	80			
Use future progressive	81			
Learn about government housing programs in your community	84			
Create a T chart to compare information	82, 85			

Scene 1: Conversation

With a partner, talk about the pictures. Listen to the conversation. Ask and answer the questions.

Pedro and Steve are talking about their plans for summer vacation.

What are you going to do this summer, Steve?

I'm going to visit Japan, China, and the Hawaiian Islands.

Wow! How are you going to go to all those places? With a credit card?

No, with this library card.

Hey, could you loan me that card?

You can get one yourself. Just ask the librarian for an application, show her some proof of residence, and she'll give you a library card. Then you can borrow books and videotapes and travel the world too!

Questions

What is Steve going to do this summer?

How is he going to do it?

What does Pedro want Steve to do?

What does Steve tell Pedro about the library card?

Do you have a library card?

Where is your local library?

Vocabulary

Look at the words. Listen to your teacher. Say the words.

applicant = person who fills out the application
to borrow = to use something that isn't yours for a short time
to loan = to lend = to give something you own to someone else for a short time

     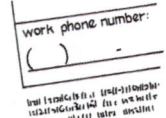

| librarian | library card | proof of residence | residential address | signature | leave it blank |

Exercise 1 Steve went to the library to find a book. Match the words in Column A with the meanings in Column B. Write the letter.

COLUMN A	COLUMN B
__f__ 1. a library card	a. to use something and then return it
____ 2. proof of residence	b. to give something for short time use and then get it back
____ 3. to loan	c. don't write anything
____ 4. to borrow	d. the address of your home
____ 5. leave it blank	e. papers showing the address of your home
____ 6. residential address	f. a card that allows you to borrow books

Listening

Exercise 2 Pedro is filling out the application to get a library card. Listen to his conversation with the librarian. Complete the application.

After You Listen
Compare your answers with a partner.

Your Turn

With a partner, use Pedro's application to ask and answer these questions. Does Pedro have a Social Security number? Does Pedro have a work telephone number? Is Pedro's residential address the same as or different from his mailing address? Does Pedro's parent need to sign his application? Share your answers with the class.

Spencer Public Library
LIBRARY CARD APPLICATION

Please Print

Applicant's Social Security Number (None)	First Name	Full Middle Name Gomez	Last Name

Mailing address

Avenue

City Spencer	State	Zip Code

Telephone	Birth date
HM _____ WK: _____	

RESIDENTIAL ADDRESS IF DIFFERENT FROM ABOVE

Residential Address

City	State	Zip Code

Would you like to receive information about library services?
____ ✔ ____ Yes _____ No

Signature of Applicant	Signature of Parent or Guardian if applicant is under age 16
X	X

SPOTLIGHT on Demonstrative Adjectives

Singular

This book is about California.

Singular

That book is about Japan.

Plural

These books are about Mexico.

Plural

Those books are about China.

Use **this** and **these** before nouns = near
Use **that** and **those** before nouns = not near

Exercise 3 Read about the books Pedro found at the library. Complete the sentences. Write the correct word on the line. Use <u>this, that, these, and those</u>.

1. _____This_____ book is about Mexico.

2. _____ book is about Alaska.

3. _____ tapes are for children.

4. _____ tapes are for adults.

5. _____ dictionary is used to look up the meaning of words.

Exercise 4 In your notebook, write sentences about some things on your desk and about some things on the teacher's desk. For example, write, "These pencils are mine. Those pencils are the teacher's. This notebook is black. That notebook is blue."

Pair Work

Listen to the conversation between Steve and Pedro. Then practice it with a partner.

Pedro: Is that book about China?

Steve: Yes, it is. I borrowed this book from the library yesterday.

Pedro: Are those papers your homework from class?

Steve: No, they're not. I printed these papers from the computer at the library yesterday. These papers are about China too.

Talk About It

In a group, talk with other students about your personal items or about things in the classroom. For example, say, "Is that book for your English class?" "Yes, this book is for my English class."

Reading for Real

Steve and Pedro went to the library together. They read this flyer about services the library offers.

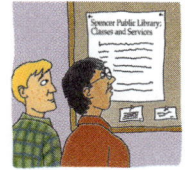

Spencer Public Library
Classes and Services

The following services and classes are FREE to the public. Registration is necessary. Call 588-3718 for more information or to register.

Youth Services (for ages 2–12)

Story times   Music Programs
Class visits   Homework Helpers
Summer Reading

Teen Programs

Family Nights at the Library
Young Adult Summer Reading Programs
Writing Programs: Write about favorite books for other teenagers

Adult and Senior Programs

Book delivery to sick and older adults not able to come
to the library
Book Discussion Groups
Summer Reading Programs
Learning to Read Programs
Introduction to the Computer Classes
Internet Classes

Exercise 5 Pedro is surprised at the classes at the library. Read the questions below. Look for the answers in the flyer above. Circle the letter of the best answer.

1. Which class is free?
   a. Homework Helpers
   b. Book Discussion Groups
   c. both

2. Which group can visit the library together?
   a. classes of children
   b. classes of seniors
   c. both

3. Which class is NOT offered for adults?
   a. Learning to Read
   b. Internet Classes
   c. Music Class

4. Who does the library deliver books to?
   a. children
   b. old and sick people
   c. families

5. Which group can write about their favorite books for a writing program?
   a. teenagers
   b. families
   c. seniors

6. Which program is offered to everyone?
   a. Internet Classes
   b. Learning to Read Programs
   c. Summer Reading Programs

Talk About It

In a group, ask and answer these questions.
Do you know about any special programs or classes at a library? Do you go to the library for special services or classes? Which class or service in the flyer above is interesting to you?

With a partner, talk about the pictures. Listen to the conversation.
Ask and answer the questions.

Steve is at the library. He is looking for a book about China.

Excuse, me. Could you please show me some books about China?

Sure, I can show them to you. The travel books are here in the nonfiction section.

Nonfiction

You can check out these books, but you can't check out that atlas. It's a reference book.

ATLAS

CHINA TODAY

The due date is the 29th. The fine for overdue books is twenty-five cents a day.

Thanks. I'm going to return these books on time!

LIBRARY

CHINA TODAY

Questions

What is Steve looking for?

Where can he find them?

Why can't he check out the atlas?

How much is the fine for overdue books?

What is Steve going to do?

Have you ever checked out a book from the library?

Why can't a reference book be checked out?

Vocabulary

Look at the words. Listen to your teacher. Say the words.

on time = at the correct time

to check out a book = to borrow a book from the library

due date

overdue

library fine

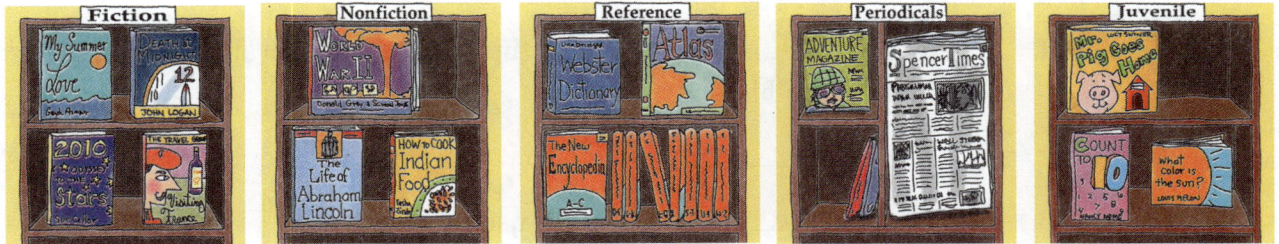

Exercise 6 Steve is looking for a new book to read. Complete the sentences. Use the words above to help you. Write the correct word on the line.

1. You can find books about the true lives of people in the _____*nonfiction*_____ section of the library.
2. An atlas has maps of the world. You can find it in the _____ section, but you can't check it out.
3. You can read important news in **Newsweek**. You can find this magazine in the _____ section.
4. **Star Wars** is a science fiction book about adventures in space. The story is not true. You can find it in the _____ section.
5. **Peter Rabbit** is a book for children. It's in the _____ section.

Listening

Exercise 7 Listen to the conversations in the library. Write the kinds of books Pedro, Steve and Tam are looking for and the section where they can find the books.

	Kind of Book	Section
Pedro		
Steve		
Tam		

After You Listen Compare your answers with a partner.

Your Turn

With a partner, ask and answer questions about where to find library books. Look at the bookshelves at the top of the page. For example, ask "Where can I find a history book?" "You can find a history book in the nonfiction section."

SPOTLIGHT on Could and Would for Requests

Could I use a computer at 2:00?	**Could** you help me with this application?
Could I check out this book?	**Would** you check out this book for me?
Could I use the copy machine?	**Would** you show me how to use the copy machine?
Use **could** to politely ask permission.	Use **could** or **would** to politely ask someone for a favor.

Exercise 8 Pedro wants to learn about the library. Complete the questions. Write the correct words on the line. Use <u>could I, could you</u> or <u>would you</u>.

1. _____<u>Could I</u>_____ check out this book about Abraham Lincoln? I want to learn about American history.

2. _____ give me some information about library services?

3. _____ sign up to use the computer? I want to go on the Internet.

4. _____ show me the nonfiction section?

5. _____ help me find a book about Mexico?

6. _____ sign up for the class on Tuesday?

7. _____ tell me how much the fine is for this overdue book?

8. _____ show me where to return these books?

Exercise 9 In your notebook, write a question to make a request or ask a favor for each of the following:

1. You are at the library. You want the librarian to show you the reference section.
2. You want to use the computer at 3:00.
3. You want the librarian to give you some information about computer classes.
4. You want to get an application for a library card.
5. You need to pay a fine for an overdue book.
6. You need the librarian to help you find a book about China.

Pair Work

Listen to the conversation between Steve and the librarian. Then practice it with a partner.

Steve:　　　Excuse me. Could you help me find some information about Mexico?

Librarian:　I sure could. The travel books are in the nonfiction section.

Steve:　　　Could I check out this book about Mexico?

Librarian:　Certainly. I'm happy to help you.

Your Turn

With a partner, practice making requests and asking for favors. For example, ask "Could I borrow your pencil?" "Sure." "Would you loan me your eraser?" "Certainly. It's no problem."

SPOTLIGHT on Indirect Objects

I need to send the <u>book</u> to **you**.
Could you buy the <u>book</u> for **me**?
She gave a <u>library card</u> to **him**.
She made a <u>library card</u> for **her**.
She showed the <u>fiction section</u> to **us**.
He read the <u>chapter</u> to **them**.

Sometimes there are two objects in a sentence. A <u>direct object</u> receives the action of the verb. An **indirect object** tells to or for whom or what the direct object is intended.

I need to send **you** the <u>book</u>.
Could you buy **me** the <u>book</u>?
She gave **him** a <u>library card</u>.
She made **her** a <u>library card</u>.
She showed **us** the <u>fiction section</u>.
He read **them** the <u>chapter</u>.

With verbs of communication and exchange such as **give, read, send, tell, write, bring, buy, show, make** or **teach**, the indirect object can go before or after the direct object. When the indirect object is before the direct object, do not use **to** or **for**.

Exercise 10 Steve asked Pedro what happened at the library. Complete the sentences. Use <u>me</u>, <u>him</u>, <u>her</u>, <u>us</u> or <u>them</u>. Write the correct word on the line.

1. What did the librarian give you?
    She gave _____ me _____ an application.

2. Did you give John the information?
    Yes, I gave _____ the information.

3. Did the library loan Maria the book?
    Yes, the library loaned _____ the book.

4. Did he show you and Lynn the computers?
    Yes, he showed _____ the computers.

5. What did the library send to Maria and Lynn?
    The library sent _____ information about the computer classes.

Exercise 11 In your notebook, rewrite the sentences on the right in Exercise 10. Change the place of the indirect object. Use <u>to</u> in the new sentences. For example, write, "She gave an application to me."

Talk About It

In a group, ask and answer questions. Use indirect objects. For example, ask, "Did the teacher give the book to you?" " Yes, she gave me the book."

Organizing Your Ideas

Books in the library are organized in different ways. Fiction books are organized alphabetically by the authors' last names. Multiple books by the same author are organized alphabetically by title. Look at the mystery books listed below. Rewrite the list in the correct alphabetical order. For titles that begin with *The* or *A*, look at the second word to decide the alphabetical order.

M is for Murder by Sue Grafton

Murder on the Titanic by James Walker

The Beach House by James Patterson

On the Street Where You Live
     by Mary Higgins Clark

A Small Death in Lisbon by Robert Wilson

L.A. Dead by Stuart Woods

Killing Floor by Lee Child

Black Spider by James Patterson

Author's Last Name	Title of Book
Child	Killing Floor

Nonfiction books are organized by topic. In the library, first find the section for the kind of nonfiction books you want to read, and then look at the titles. Look at titles of the nonfiction books in the list below. Write the book titles in the correct sections.

The Way to Cook

Russia and Its Neighbors

Soccer Techniques

Tennis Success

World War II

The Mountains of China

Easy Sewing Lessons

How to Plant a Garden

The Revolution of 1776

Mexico

The Vietnam War

Baseball in America

Geography Books	Sports Books	History Books	Home Economics Books

Talk About It

In a group, look at the lists of books. Circle the ones you would like to read. Ask and answer these questions. Do you like to read nonfiction books? Which ones? Do you like to read fiction? Do you read in both English and your native language?

Issues and Answers

Pedro just got his library card but he has a problem. Read the letter and Abdul's advice. Then talk with other students about the advice. Do you agree? What other advice can you give?

Ask Abdul and Anita

DEAR ABDUL,

I just got a library card, and I want to check out some books. I think reading books can help me learn English. I learned about the sections of the library, and I know how to check out books, but there's one problem. I don't speak English very well, and it's difficult to ask the librarian for help. I want to read about places around the world. I want to find some <u>easy</u> English books. What can I do?

—Pedro Mendoza

DEAR PEDRO,

You're right. Reading books is a good way to learn English. You can try looking for books in the Juvenile Section. Children's books are easy to read, and some of them have tapes you can listen to while you read. You can find children's books about sports, science, and other interesting topics. You can also ask a friend or classmate to go to the library with you and help you find books. Good luck!

—Abdul

Your Turn

Pedro needs some help at the library. What advice can you give him?

Step 1: With a partner, make a list of things Pedro can do or read at the library to help him learn English. Include fiction and nonfiction books. Use your chart from page 94 for ideas.

Step 2: Role-play a conversation between Pedro and the librarian about the things in Step 1. What questions can Pedro ask the librarian? What suggestions can the librarian make to Pedro?

Step 3: Share the list you made in Step 1 with the class. Practice the conversation you made for Pedro and the librarian with another group or the class.

Community Involvement

Libraries offer many services. You can check out books and videotapes, and sometimes you can also take classes. You can use the computers to prepare papers for school or to search the Internet. There are many programs for children, young people and adults.

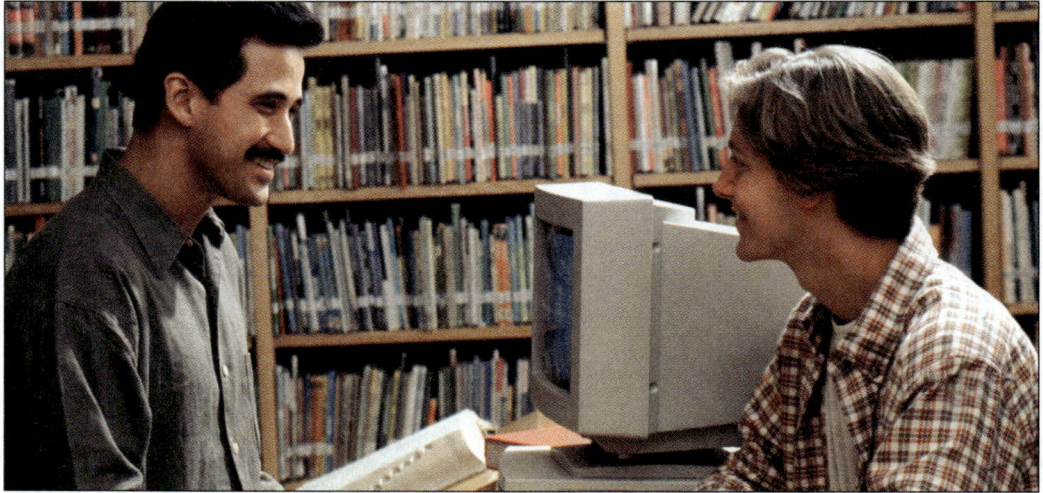

Your Turn

With a partner, talk about your library experiences. Do you have a library card? Did you use the library in your native country? How did you use it? Was it the same or different from the library in the United States?

Community Action

Step 1: With a partner, find the library closest to your home. Look in the telephone book and write the name, address, and telephone number of the library below.

· Name of the library _____
· Address _____
· Telephone number _____

Step 2: With your partner, look on the library web site and find the answers to the questions below. Or, you can call or visit the library to find the information. If you don't have a library card, go to the library and get one!

· What days and hours is the library open? _____
· For how many days can I check out a book? _____
· What is the fine for overdue books? _____
· Do you have books or videotapes in my language? _____
· What proof of residence do I need to get a library card? _____

Talk About It

In a group, talk about the information you learned about the library in your neighborhood. What is the best thing about the library in your community? How many students in your group have library cards? How many students want to get them? Share your answers with the class.

💡 Wrap Up

Steve and Pedro found books they liked in the library. Which books do you like? In a group, choose books for a small library. Your library only has 12 books. Each person should choose three books. They can be books you know, or books from this unit on pages 91 and 94. You can also make your own title for an interesting book. Write the titles of the books below.

Library Book List

1.	5.	9.
2.	6.	10.
3.	7.	11.
4.	8.	12.

Now it's time to visit the libraries. Find a partner from another group. Role-play a librarian and a person who wants to check out a book. Use words from this unit, demonstrative adjectives, **could** and **would,** and indirect objects if you can. For example:

A: Excuse me, could you help me? I'm looking for a book about tennis.

B: I'm sorry. We don't have a book about tennis. Would you like a book about soccer? This book is <u>All About Soccer</u>.

A: Could you show me some mystery books?

B: Sure. We have <u>Murder at Sea</u> and <u>Big Mystery</u>.

A: I'll take <u>Big Mystery</u>.

When a person "checks out" a book, cross it off your list. Then change partners and role-play the conversation again. Visit four or five "libraries" and role-play more conversations about books.

Think About Learning

Check (✔) to show your learning in this unit. Then write one more thing you learned.

SKILLS / STRUCTURES	PAGE	EASY 😊	SO-SO 😐	DIFFICULT 😟
Talk about library cards and how to use them	86, 90			
Understand how to fill out an application for a library card	87			
Use **this, that, these,** and **those** before nouns	88			
Read and talk about library services	89			
Understand a conversation with a librarian	91			
Use **could** and **would** for requests	92			
Use indirect and direct objects	93			
Create a chart to organize your ideas	94			
Learn about the library in your community	96			

Unit 9   You're Hired!

With a partner, talk about the pictures. Listen to the conversation. Ask and answer the questions.

Houshang is looking for a job. He talks to Mr. Petersen, the owner of Petersen's Auto Repair.

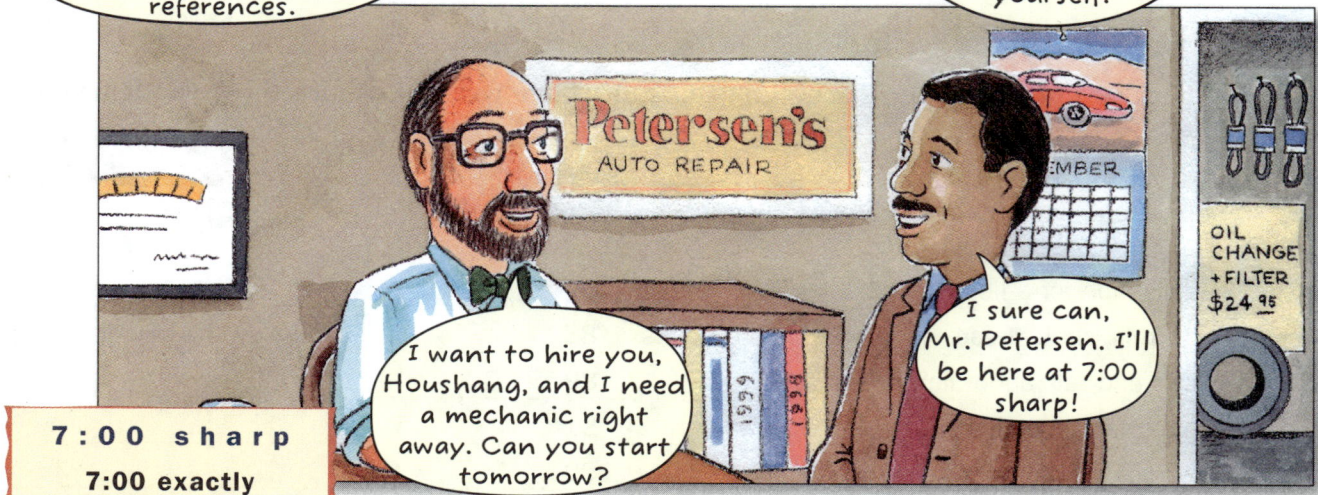

So you're interested in a job as a mechanic. Do you have mechanical skills?

Yes, I do, Mr. Petersen. I know how to fix brakes, and I can repair motors too. I was a mechanic in my country for five years. Here's my résumé. I have good references.

Well, I'm very dependable. I learn quickly, and I like to work with people.

Sounds like you have the experience and qualifications for the job. Tell me a little more about yourself.

I want to hire you, Houshang, and I need a mechanic right away. Can you start tomorrow?

I sure can, Mr. Petersen. I'll be here at 7:00 sharp!

OIL CHANGE + FILTER $24.95

7:00 sharp
7:00 exactly

Questions

What kind of job is Houshang interested in?

Does he have mechanical skills?

How much experience does Houshang have?

Why do you think Mr. Petersen wants to hire Houshang?

Do you have job experience? How much?

What job skills do you have?

Vocabulary

Look at the words and pictures. Listen to your teacher. Say the words.

dependable = hardworking, always comes to work
experience = work in the past
mechanical skills = things a mechanic knows how to do

right away = very soon or immediately
to know how to = to understand the way to do something

**assembler;
to assemble
electronics;
to connect wires**

**computer
programmer; to use
the computer; to do
data processing**

**landscaper; to mow
the lawn; to trim
shrubs**

job qualifications =
skills and other
things you need to
get a job

**mechanic; to fix
brakes; to repair
cars and trucks**

**office assistant; to
make copies; to do
data processing**

**seamstress; to sew;
to make clothes**

to hire = to offer
a job

Exercise 1 Houshang's friends have many different jobs and skills. Complete the sentences. Use the words above to help you. Write the correct words on the lines.

Mario is an assembler. He knows how to **(1)** <u>assemble electronics</u>. He can

(2) _____ too. Donato is a landscaper. He knows how to mow lawns

and **(3)** _____. Yoko is an office assistant. She knows how to

(4) _____, and she can **(5)** _____ too. Houshang is a

mechanic. He has mechanical skills. He knows how to **(6)** _____.

Listening

Exercise 2 Listen to Houshang's friends talk about their jobs. Take notes. Complete the chart below. Write each person's job, skills, and experience.

Name	Job	Skills	Experience
Donato	landscaper		
Yoko			
Mario			

After You Listen Compare your answers with a partner.

Your Turn

With a partner, make sentences about the information in Exercise 2. For example, say, "Donato is a landscaper. He can _____ and _____.
He has _____ years of experience."

SPOTLIGHT on Review Verb + Infinitive

Some verbs are followed by infinitives.

I **like to work** with people.
You **had to work** yesterday.
She **wanted to be** a teacher.
He **knew how to repair** motors.
It **needs to be** finished by Monday.

We **hope to retire** young.
You will **need to learn** more English.
They **plan to go** on Monday.

To talk about the past or future, change the first verb to past tense or future tense. Do not change the verb after **to.**

Correct: I liked to ride in a car.   Incorrect: I liked to rode in a car.

Exercise 3 Read about Houshang's friends and family. Write the correct words on the line. Use present, past, or future forms of the words in parentheses ( ) and the infinitive forms of the words below. Look for clues in the sentences to help you.

fill out	punch in	work	travel	use
be	punch out	take	read	start

1. Martha is a kindergarten teacher. She **(like)** _____likes to work_____ with children.

2. Houshang's brother is looking for a job. He **(need)** _____ an application.

3. Tracy was a librarian. She **(like)** _____ books.

4. I am a student. I **(need)** _____ more English.

5. Bert **(plan)** _____ college next year.

6. Lee will begin a new job tomorrow. He **(have)** _____ on time.

Exercise 4 In your notebook, write three sentences about work you like to do, three sentences about work you know how to do, and three sentences about things you need to do to get the job you want. Use the sentences in Exercise 3 to help you.

Pair Work

Listen to the conversation between Houshang and his friend Marcy. Then practice it with a partner.

Marcy: What kind of job do you want to have?
Houshang: I want to have a job as a mechanic.
Marcy: What are your qualifications?
Houshang: I know how to repair motors and I like to work on cars. How about you?
Marcy: I want to find a job as a seamstress. I like to sew and I know how to make dresses.

Talk About It

In a group, talk about jobs you want and your qualifications for the jobs. For example, say, "I want to be a cook. I like to prepare food and I know how to make Chinese food."

Reading for Real

Houshang's friend Marcy saw this article in the newspaper. She thinks the job interview tips can help her get the job she wants. Read the tips from the newspaper.

Job Interview Tips

Before the Interview:

Think about the questions on a job application. Bring information to answer the questions. You should have names, addresses, and telephone numbers from your old jobs and schools too. Practice speaking about the information on the application with a friend. Answer questions about your job experience and job skills. Before you leave your home, you should be clean and neat. Wear nice clothes.

At the Interview:

Smile. Stand straight. Give a firm handshake. Look in the interviewer's eyes when you speak. Don't be shy. Learn and use the interviewer's name. Ask questions when you don't understand. Be honest. If the answer to a question is no, don't lie and say yes. Add a few good words about yourself too. For example, if the interviewer asks about your computer skills, say, "I don't know how to use a computer yet, but I can learn. I go to school, and my teacher says I'm a fast learner."

Exercise 5 Marcy is afraid to interview in English. Read the questions below. Look for the answers in the article above. Circle the letter of the best answer.

1. What information should Marcy bring to answer questions on the application?
   a. names and phone numbers from old jobs
   b. the job she wants
   c. a note from her school

2. What should Marcy practice talking about with a friend?
   a. names and phone numbers from old jobs
   b. things she learned in school
   c. her job skills and job experience

3. What should Marcy wear to the interview?
   a. clean shirt and jeans
   b. clean, nice clothes
   c. shorts and a t-shirt

4. Which of the following is not necessary at the interview?
   a. to shake hands
   b. to give a gift
   c. to be honest

5. What should Marcy NOT do at the interview?
   a. learn the interviewer's name
   b. stand up straight and smile
   c. be shy

6. Why should Marcy follow the advice in the newspaper?
   a. It will help her get the job.
   b. It will help her feel more confident.
   c. both

Talk About It

In a group, talk about going to a job interview. Do you agree with the advice in the article? Are the tips good for job interviews in your native country? What other tips do you have for preparing for an interview?

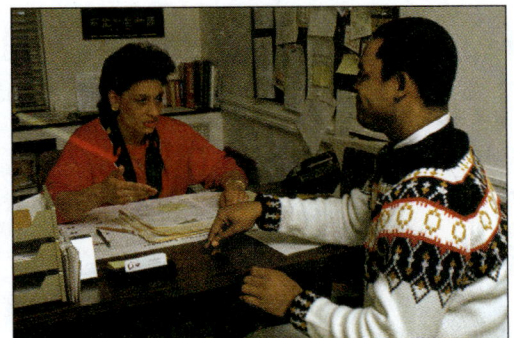

Scene 2: Conversation

With a partner, talk about the pictures. Listen to the conversation.
Ask and answer the questions.

Thank you for hiring me, Mr. Petersen. Do I have to buy a uniform or provide my own tools?

You don't have to provide your own tools or wear a uniform, but you must wear appropriate clothes. And you must wear heavy work shoes.

Are there any more company policies I need to know about?

Smoking is not permitted on the job. You mustn't smoke around the cars. And, of course, you must punch in on time.

I'll arrive on time and I won't smoke. You can count on that, Mr. Petersen.

Good. I have your résumé, but I need to check your references. Here is your W-4 form for your taxes. You have to fill it out before you start to work. Uncle Sam wants his money, you know.

to count on

to be sure about

Uncle Sam

the United States government

Questions

Does Houshang have to buy a uniform?
Does he have to provide his own tools?
Does he have to wear heavy work shoes?
Is smoking permitted on the job at Petersen's Auto Repair?

Why do you think workers at Petersen's Auto Repair mustn't smoke on the job?
Who is Uncle Sam? What money does he want? Why?

Vocabulary

Look at the words and pictures. Listen to your teacher. Say the words.

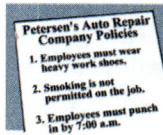    

appropriate   company   heavy work   résumé   W-4 form   not
clothes (for   policies   shoes   permitted
a mechanic)

Name	Address	Telephone	Relationship
Fred Zabaleta	621 Elm Street Harvest Springs CA 99142	310-555-6544	employer
Sandra Smith	128 Orange Street Spencer, CA 92190	310-555-5691	landlord
Betty Wells	Mid City School 892 C Street La Mesa CA 91941	619-555-4566	teacher

to provide   to wear   references
own tools   uniforms

Exercise 6 Read about the company policies where Houshang and his friends work. Complete the sentences. Use the words above to help you.

1. Sue bought a white dress because she's a nurse at Spencer Community Hospital. All the nurses at the hospital must wear _____ uniforms _____.

2. Jose bought a hammer and saw because he works for a construction company. The workers have to _____ their _____.

3. At Petersen's Auto Repair, smoking is _____ on the job.

4. Mr. Petersen had to call people Houshang worked with in the past. Houshang's _____ were very good.

5. _____ are the rules for employees at a work place.

> **withholding**
> tax deductions
> from a paycheck
>
> **allowances**
> number of people you
> count as dependents

Listening

Exercise 7 Listen to Houshang talk about his W-4 form. The form tells the company how much money to take out, or withhold, for state and federal income taxes. Write the information in the correct places on the form.

After You Listen
Compare your answers with a partner.

Your Turn

W-4 FORM

NAME (Last, First, Middle) Saifnia, Houshang Hagani

Social Security Number _____

Home Address _____ First Street, Spencer, CA 92190

Marital Status: Check One:
☐ Single ☐ Married ☐ Married, but withhold at higher single rate

1. STATE
   Total number of allowances you are claiming for this job. _____

2. FEDERAL
   Total number of allowances you are claiming for this job. _____

Houshang Saifnia _____ Date _____
Employee's Signature

With a partner, ask and answer questions about the W-4 form in Exercise 7. What is Houshang's Social Security number? Is he married? How many Federal allowances is he claiming?

SPOTLIGHT on Must, Must Not, Have to, Don't Have to

In the affirmative, **must** and **have to** are about the same:

Company employees **have to be** drug-free.

Company employees **must be** drug-free.

He **has to take** a drug test before he starts to work at the company.

He **must take** a drug test before he starts to work at the company.

In the negative, **mustn't** and **don't have to** are very different:

Mustn't means not permitted, or do not.

Workers **mustn't smoke** on the job.

Houshang **mustn't smoke** on the job.

Don't have to means not necessary.

Workers **don't have to wear** uniforms.

He **doesn't have to provide** his own tools.

Exercise 8 Houshang is trying to learn about the company policies at Petersen's Auto Repair. Complete the sentences. Write the correct word on the line. Use <u>have to, must, don't have to, doesn't have to,</u> or <u>mustn't</u>.

Houshang read the company policy manual. It says Petersen's Auto Repair Employees

(1) _____ must _____ be drug-free. Houshang (2) _____ take a

drug test before he starts to work there. Employees (3) _____ take or

sell drugs. Employees (4) _____ wear uniforms, but they

(5) _____ wear heavy work shoes for safety. (6) They

_____ to provide their own tools because the company provides them.

Employees (7) _____ be on time for work, but they

(8) _____ work overtime if they don't want to. They

(9) _____ take more than an hour for lunch and they

(10) _____ phone the company if they can't come to work because of

illness or other emergency.

Exercise 9 In your notebook, write sentences about the company policies where you work, or write about the rules at your school. Use <u>have to</u> or <u>must</u>, <u>don't have to</u> or <u>mustn't</u>.

Your Turn

With a partner, ask and answer questions about the rules you wrote in Exercise 9. Talk about things you **have to** or **must do**, things you **don't have to do**, and things you **mustn't do**.

SPOTLIGHT on Compound Sentences with And . . . too, And . . . either

Affirmative Sentences

I wash cars, **and** I clean houses **too.**

José knows how to use a computer, **and** he can communicate well, **too.**

> Use **and . . . too** to combine two affirmative sentences.

Negative Sentences

You don't have to wear a uniform, **and** you don't have to provide your own tools, **either.**

They don't know how to use a computer, **and** they can't do data processing, **either.**

> Use **and . . . either** to combine two negative sentences.

Exercise 10 Many people can do more than one thing at work. In your notebook, combine the sentences. Use <u>and . . . too</u> and <u>and . . . either</u>.

1. Carmen knows how to drive a car. She can drive a truck.
   <u>Carmen knows how to drive a car, and she can drive a truck too.</u>
2. Alfredo is strong. He is a hard worker.
3. Tony doesn't do data processing well. He can't communicate well.
4. Nora and Joseph don't have a computer. They don't do data processing either.
5. Houshang must wear heavy work shoes. He must wear safety glasses.
6. Mohammed doesn't have to come to work early. He doesn't have to work overtime.
7. Marie mustn't be late for work. She mustn't leave early.
8. I have to fill out the application. I have to fill out the W-4 form.

Exercise 11 In your notebook, write two affirmative and two negative sentences about your job skills or job experiences. Use <u>and . . . too</u> and <u>and . . . either</u>, and the sentences in Exercise 10 to help you. For example, write, "I can use the computer, and I can file papers, too. I don't have to wear a uniform and I don't have to wear heavy work shoes either."

Pair Work

Listen to the conversation between Houshang's friend Olga and an interviewer. Then practice it with a partner.

Olga:	I'm interested in a job as a cook.
Interviewer:	What are your qualifications?
Olga:	I can cook very well, and I can use kitchen equipment too.
Interviewer:	Do you know how to make bread and pizza?
Olga:	No, I don't know how to make bread, and I don't know how to make pizza either. But I learn fast, and I will be a very good cook at your restaurant.

Your Turn

With a partner, role play a conversation between a job applicant and an interviewer. Use the sentences you wrote in Exercise 11 to help you. Share your role-play with the class.

Organizing Your Ideas

Think about two jobs you know. Write the jobs in the boxes below. Next write some job skills necessary for each of the jobs in the circles. Look at the pictures on page 99 to help you.

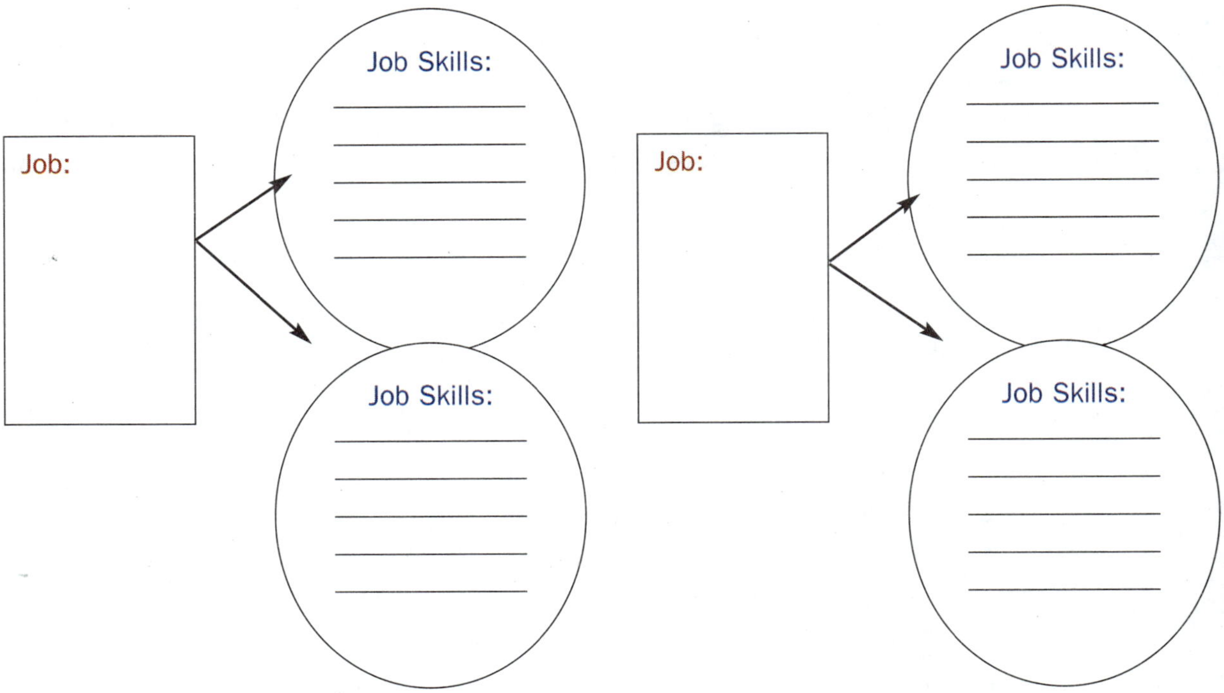

Job:

Job Skills:
_____
_____
_____
_____
_____

Job Skills:
_____
_____
_____
_____
_____

Job:

Job Skills:
_____
_____
_____
_____
_____

Job Skills:
_____
_____
_____
_____
_____

Now think about your job skills. Think about things you know how to do and the things you like to do. Write your skills in the circle below. Then think about possible jobs you can have. Write possible jobs in the boxes.

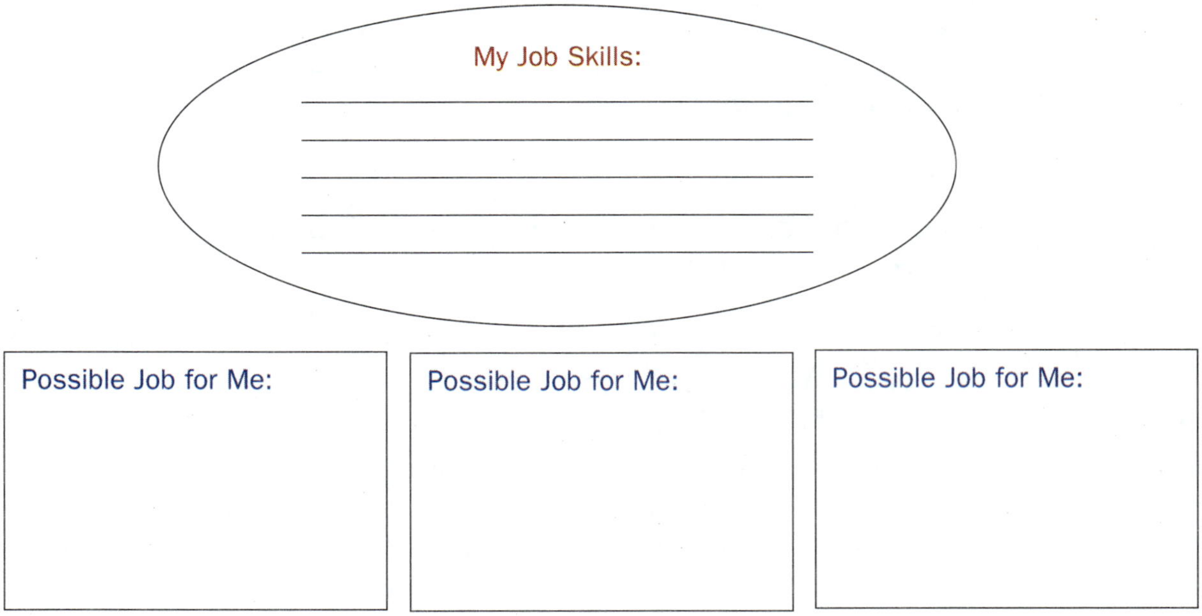

My Job Skills:
_____
_____
_____
_____
_____

Possible Job for Me:

Possible Job for Me:

Possible Job for Me:

💡 Talk About It

In a group, talk about the jobs and job skills in your first idea map. Then talk about your job skills and possible jobs for you. Do you have job skills that you don't use? Are there other possible jobs for you? Share your information with the class.

Issues and Answers

Houshang's friend Bárbara decided to write a letter asking for advice. Read the letter and Mr. Nakamura's advice. Then talk with other students about the advice. Do you agree? What other advice can you give?

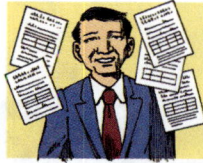

Ask Mr. Nakamura

DEAR MR. NAKAMURA,

   I am a student now. I don't have a job. In my country, I was a full-time student. Now, I want to apply for a job. What do I write on my job application about job experience? What do I say about job skills? Help!

—BÁRBARA

DEAR BÁRBARA,

   When I interviewed for my first job, I didn't have job experience either. But I had experience helping my family. Maybe you helped your family too. Did you ever help with a family business? cook? clean? babysit? Volunteer work for relatives, school, or the community is experience. And you have at least one job skill—you can read, write, and communicate in two languages!

—MR. NAKAMURA, HUMAN RESOURCES MANAGER

Your Turn

Bárbara made a list of her volunteer work experience to help her apply for jobs. You can do the same.

Step 1:   With a partner, make a list of your experience volunteering in the community or helping your family at home. Add your experience volunteering or helping your family at home to the job skills you listed on page 106.

Step 2:   Write some questions employers sometimes ask about job experience. Look at the conversations on pages 98, 100, and 105 to help you. Then practice how to answer the questions. Role-play an interview between an employer and a person looking for work. Use the list you made in Step 1 to help you answer the questions.

Step 3:   Practice your interview. Share it with the class.

Community Involvement

There are many sources for information about jobs in your community. Sometimes you can read notices about jobs on a bulletin board at a school, library, or church. And many businesses put "Help Wanted" signs in their windows to tell people about job openings. You can read the want ads in the newspaper, and you can search for information on the Internet, too. You can find information about jobs at the Department of Employment Development. Don't forget to talk to your friends about job openings at their workplaces.

Your Turn

With a partner, talk about your experience learning about job openings. Did you have a job before in your native country or in the United States? How did you learn about the job opening? How did you apply?

Community Action

Step 1: With a partner, talk about how you can find information about jobs. In your notebook, make a list of sources for information about jobs in your community. (Remember to ask friends and family members with jobs.) Look in the telephone book for the address and telephone number of the Department of Work Development in your community and write it here.

Department of Work Development

Address _____

Telephone number _____

Step 2: Use the sources you listed in Step 1. Find information about job openings. In your notebook, make a chart like the one below. Write the job information you find out from your sources in the chart.

Source of Information	Job Opening	Business
Sign in window	Dishwasher	Fred's Pizza Place
My friend, Josefina	Housekeeper	Best Sleep Hotel

Talk About It

In a group, talk about the sources of information you found and the job openings they told you about. What is the easiest way to find work? How did most people in your group find work? Are you going to apply for any of the jobs you found? Why or why not?

Wrap Up

Imagine you are starting your own business. Decide what kind of business you want to start. In your notebook, make three idea maps like the one below. In each map, write one job opening you need to fill and the qualifications people need for that job. For example, employees for a restaurant might include a cook, a waitress, and a cashier.

Kind of business _____

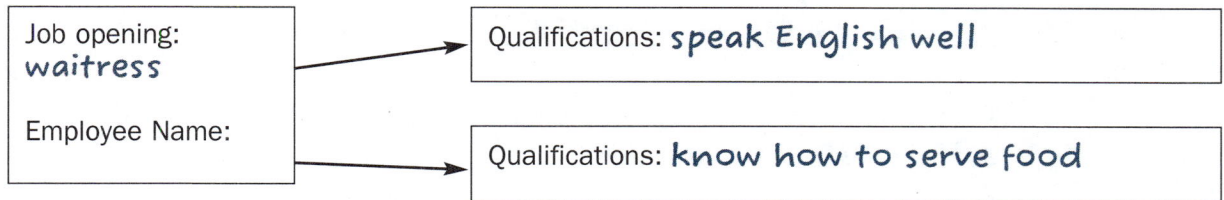

Job opening: waitress **Employee Name:**	**Qualifications:** speak English well
	Qualifications: know how to serve food

Next, work with a partner. Tell your partner about your business, the job openings you have, and the qualifications people need to have for each job. Then role-play a job interview. One person is looking for a job. One person is going to hire a worker. Look at the conversations on pages 98 and 105 to help you. Use words from this unit, verbs with infinitives, **and . . . too** and **and . . . either, must, mustn't, have to,** and **don't have to,** if you can. For example:

> **A:** I want to apply for a job as a waitress.
>
> **B:** You must have experience serving food. Do you have experience?
>
> **A:** Yes. I was a waitress in my native country, and in the United States too.
>
> **B:** Can you speak English well?
>
> **A:** My English is not perfect, but I am taking classes to learn better English.
>
> **B:** Good. You can start work on Monday.

Change partners and role-play more job interviews. Talk to as many people as you need to fill your job openings. Write the names of the people you hire for each job in your idea maps. Share your idea maps with the class.

Think About Learning

Check (✔) to show your learning in this unit. Then write one more thing you learned.

SKILLS / STRUCTURES	PAGE	EASY 😊	SO-SO 😐	DIFFICULT 😧
Talk about things you know how to do	98			
Understand conversations about job skills	99			
Use infinitives	100			
Read about interview tips	101			
Talk about company policies	102			
Fill out a W-4 form	103			
Use **must, mustn't** and **don't have to**	104			
Use **and . . . to** and **and . . . either**	105			
Create an idea map to organize your ideas about job skills and jobs	106			
Locate sources of information about jobs in your community	108			

Scene 1: Conversation

With a partner, talk about the pictures. Listen to the conversation. Ask and answer the questions.

Lien is taking the bus to a job interview. She gives a five-dollar bill to the bus driver to pay for the bus fare. She asks the bus driver for information.

Does this bus go downtown?

No, it doesn't. You should take the number 7 bus and get a bus transfer. Change at Elm Street to Route 15. By the way, you must have the exact change for the bus fare. If you use the bus a lot, you might want to get a monthly bus pass. That'll save you a lot of money.

Thanks for the information. Is there a change machine around here?

No, there isn't, but you might be able to get change at Save More Pharmacy.

I could also try the Clean Easy Laundromat. They probably have a change machine. Thanks.

I ought to learn more about the public transportation in this city. I'm planning to live here for a long time!

By the way is used to introduce extra information in a conversation

Questions

Where does Lien want to go?

What bus should she take?

What does Lien need to pay for the bus?

Did you take the bus in your native country? Did you need exact change?

Do you take the bus now? Do you have any problems using the transit system?

Vocabulary

Look at the words and pictures. Listen to your teacher. Say the words.

| bus fare | change machine | destination | transfer | bus transit center = the office for the bus company |

cross street = a street that crosses the street you are on
monthly bus pass = a card you can use to travel on the bus for one month
present location = where you are now

probably = more than 50% sure
to get around = to make short trips within a city
to make change = to return any extra money you received

Your Words

_____

_____

Exercise 1 Lien is learning about the bus system. Circle the letter of the phrase that best completes each sentence.

1. Your **destination** is
   a. the bus station.
   b. your home address.
   c. the place you want to go.

2. **Bus fare** is
   a. money for a bus ride.
   b. the distance you travel.
   c. the time you travel.

3. Bus drivers **don't make change.** This means
   a. they don't help you change buses.
   b. they always drive the same way.
   c. they don't return extra fare money.

4. To use a **transfer** means to
   a. pay for a bus fare.
   b. change to a different bus.
   c. arrive at your destination.

5. A **cross street** is
   a. a street that crosses another street.
   b. a bus stop.
   c. a destination.

6. There is **probably** a change machine near the bus station. This means
   a. you can be 100% sure to find one.
   b. you can be 50% sure to find one.
   c. you can be 90% sure to find one.

Listening

Exercise 2 Many people call the bus company to ask questions. Listen to these conversations about taking the bus. Read the sentences. Circle <u>yes</u> or <u>no</u>.

Caller #1 Ivan	The caller is on Vermont Street.	Yes	No
	The caller knows the name of the cross street.	Yes	No
Caller #2 Hanna	The bus ride costs $1.65.	Yes	No
	The driver gave change.	Yes	No
Caller #3 Margo	The woman paid another 35 cents.	Yes	No
	She got a transfer for Bus 10.	Yes	No

After You Listen Compare your answers with a partner.

Your Turn

With a partner, correct the sentences about information in Exercise 2. Change the sentences you marked "no" to negative sentences. For example, say "The caller doesn't know the name of the cross street."

SPOTLIGHT on Should and Ought To

I **should** get a bus pass.
He **should** get a bus pass.
We **should** call the bus transit station.

You **shouldn't** play your radio on the bus.
She **shouldn't** use her cell phone on the bus.
They **shouldn't** talk too loudly on the bus.

I **ought to** get a bus pass.
He **ought to** get a bus pass.
We **ought to** call the bus transit station.

You **ought not to** play your radio on the bus.
She **ought not to** use her cell phone on the bus.
They **ought not to** talk too loudly on the bus.

Use **should** and **ought to** to express opinions or give advice in statements. In questions, use **should**.

Exercise 3 Read about what Lien should do on the transit system. Write <u>should</u>, <u>shouldn't</u>, <u>ought to</u>, or <u>ought not to</u> on the lines below.

1. You <u>should/ought to</u> have exact change for the bus fare.

2. You _____ smoke on the subway.

3. Lien _____ call the transit station for bus route information.

4. Lien and Juan _____ take bus 15 downtown.

5. Lien _____ talk to the bus driver while he's driving.

6. Lien _____ get a bus pass to save money.

7. Lien _____ miss the bus or she'll be late for her job interview.

8. They _____ play their radios on the bus.

Exercise 4 In your notebook, write sentences about things you should or shouldn't do on the bus, train or in any public place. For example, write, "I should have exact change for the bus fare." You can use <u>ought to</u> and <u>ought not to</u> in place of <u>should</u> and <u>shouldn't</u>. For example, "I ought to have exact change for the bus fare."

Pair Work

Listen to the conversation between Lien and Juan. Then practice it with a partner.

Lien: I need to go downtown for a job interview. Which bus should I take?

Juan: I don't know. You should call the bus station.

Lien: What's the phone number?

Juan: I don't know that either. You should look up the number in the Yellow Pages and keep it with you. You shouldn't talk to strangers about bus information.

Talk About It

In a group, talk about some things you should and shouldn't do to get around in the city. Use the sentences you wrote in Exercise 4 to help you. For example, say, "You should have exact change for bus fares. You shouldn't smoke on the train."

Reading for Real

Lien just got a new job. She takes the train from her home in Irvine to her job in Los Angeles. She needs to be at work by 8:45 A.M. She leaves work at 4:45 P.M. and returns to her home in Irvine.

To Los Angeles Train Numbers	A.M. 603	681	683	605
San Juan Capistrano	5:44			7:15
Irvine	5:56	6:40	7:09	7:28
Santa Ana	6:08	6:52	7:21	
Anaheim	6:17	6:59	7:28	7:49
Fullerton	6:25	7:07	7:36	7:57
Santa Fe Springs	6:34	7:16	7:45	8:05
Commerce	6:53			8:24
L.A. Union Station	7:04	7:46	8:15	8:35

From Los Angeles Train Numbers	P.M. 604	688	606	608
L.A. Union Station	4:35	4:55	5:37	6:26
Commerce	4:51		5:53	
Santa Fe Springs	5:01	5:21	6:03	6:49
Fullerton	5:10	5:30	6:12	6:58
Anaheim	5:18	5:38	6:20	7:07
Orange	5:22	5:42	6:24	7:11
Santa Ana	5:26	5:48	6:28	7:15
Irvine	5:37	6:01	6:39	7:26
San Juan Capistrano	5:49		6:52	7:38

Exercise 5 Lien is looking for trains that are best for her schedule. Read the questions below. Look for the answers in the schedules above. Circle the letter of the best answer.

1. What time is the latest Lien needs to get on the train in Irvine?
   a. 7:28
   b. 6:40
   c. 7:09

2. If she takes train 605, what time will she arrive in L.A.'s Union Station?
   a. 8:24
   b. 8:35
   c. 8:15

3. If she takes train 605, how long will she be on the train in the morning?
   a. 1 hour
   b. 1 hour, 29 minutes
   c. 1 hour, 7 minutes

4. What time will the 4:55 train from L.A. arrive in Irvine?
   a. 5:48
   b. 4:55
   c. 6:01

5. When is the last train she can take to return to Irvine?
   a. 6:26
   b. 5:37
   c. 4:55

6. If Lien works until 5:30, what train can she take home?
   a. Train number 688
   b. Train number 606
   c. Train number 604

Talk About It

In a group, ask and answer these questions about the public transportation system in the United States. Do you use public transportation? How often? How is the public transportation system in the United States different from in your native country?

**With a partner, talk about the pictures. Listen to the conversation.
Ask and answer the questions.**

Lien is talking to her father. She wants some advice about how to get to work.

Questions

What is Lien thinking about?
Which is more expensive, the bus or the train?
What is the best kind of transportation for Lien to use?
What transportation might Lien be able to use someday?

Do you use public transportation? Is it fast? Is it expensive?
What's the best way to travel in your city?

Vocabulary

Look at the words. Listen to your teacher. Say the words.

convenient = close or fast and easy
advantage = a good thing
disadvantage = a bad thing

private transportation =
a vehicle owned by
one person

public transportation =
a vehicle used by all
people

to commute = to
travel from home to
work and back again

Exercise 6 Lien and her father talked about the different types of transportation in the city. Match the words in Column A with the definitions in Column B. Write the letter.

COLUMN A

_a_ 1. advantages
_____ 2. disadvantages
_____ 3. private transportation
_____ 4. public transportation
_____ 5. to commute
_____ 6. convenient

COLUMN B

a. good, helpful things about an idea or situation
b. to travel to and from work
c. vehicle owned by one person or family
d. transportation used by all people, such as buses, planes and trains
e. nearby, close, easy to use
f. bad things about an idea or situation

Listening

Exercise 7 Lien is thinking about buying a car. Listen to the conversation between Lien and her friends. Take notes. Write the correct information in the chart below.

Speaker	Type of transportation	Advantages	Disadvantages
Ali	Bus		
Greg			
Heidi			

After You Listen Compare your answers with a partner.

Your Turn

With a partner, ask and answer these questions. How do you commute to work or school? Do you take public or private transportation? Which do you think is more convenient? Why?

SPOTLIGHT on May and Might

I **might** take the train to work, or I **might** drive. I'm not sure yet.

Lien **might** take the train to work, or she **might** take the bus. She's not sure yet.

We **might** buy a new car, or we **might** buy a used car. We really can't decide.

I **may** take the train to work, or I **may** drive. I'm not sure yet.

Lien **may** take the train to work, or she **may** take the train. She's not sure yet.

We **may** buy a new car, or we **may** buy a used car. We really can't decide.

May and **might** have the same meaning. Use these words to talk about possibilities in the future. Use the base form of the verb after **may** and **might**.

Correct: I might take the train.
Incorrect: I might to take the train.

Exercise 8 Lien's coworkers use many different types of transportation. Complete the sentences. Use <u>may</u> or <u>might</u> and the words below. Write the correct word on the line.

| read | buy | ride | drive | visit | take | walk | go |

1. Greg _____ might buy _____ a new car, or he _____ a used car. He's trying to decide.

2. Tam _____ the train, or he _____ the bus to San Francisco. He 's not sure yet.

3. Pedro _____ his bicycle to work, or he _____ his motorcycle.

4. Maria _____ to the supermarket on the corner, or she _____ to the park. She thinks walking is good exercise.

5. Mario just bought a new car. Next weekend he _____ to Los Angeles, or he _____ to Santa Barbara.

6. Lien plans to do lots of reading on the train. Tomorrow she _____ a book or she _____ the newspaper. She's not sure yet.

Exercise 9 In your notebook, write about things you might do in the near future. For example, write, "I might take the bus to school tomorrow, or I might walk to school."

Your Turn

With a partner, ask and answer questions about your travel plans in the future. Use the sentences you wrote in Exercise 9 to help you. For example, "Are you going to take a vacation during semester break?" "I'm not sure. I might visit my family in Santa Ana or I might stay home."

SPOTLIGHT on Can and To Be Able

Past

I **could ride** a bike when I was 10, but I **couldn't drive** a car.

They **were able to take** the bus to school, but they **weren't able to take** the train.

Present

I **can drive** a car now, but I **can't buy** one.

They **may be able to ride** the bus to work today. They **may not be able to ride** the train.

Future

I **can buy** a used car next year, but I **can't buy** a new one.

They'll **be able to take** the train and the bus to work next month. They **won't be able to drive.**

Can, could and **be able to** have the same meaning. Use **be able to** in place of **can** with words like **should, may, might, must/must not, have to/don't have to, need to, want to, like to,** and **be going to.**

Exercise 10 Some of Lien's coworkers use public transportation. Use the past, present or future forms of <u>to be able to</u> or the past or present forms of <u>can</u> to fill in the blanks.

1. Lien might _____ **be able to** _____ take the train to work.

2. Mario **(not)** _couldn't /wasn't able to_ get to work on time yesterday because he missed the bus.

3. Juan **(not)** _____ buy a car last year. He had to take the bus.

4. Tam should _____ take the bus to school every day. There's a bus stop near his house.

5. There isn't a bus stop near Yoko's house so she **(not)** _____ take the bus to work. She has to walk or ask a friend to pick her up.

6. Juan **(not)** _____ take the train to the beach tomorrow because he's going to take his mother to the doctor's office.

Exercise 11 In your notebook, write sentences about things you could or couldn't do in the past, things you can or can't do now, and things you will be able to do in the future. For example, write "I can't afford a car now, but I'll be able to buy one next year."

Pair Work

Listen to the conversation between Lien and Hai. Then practice it with a partner.

Lien: Can you drive me to work tomorrow at 9:00?

Hai: I sure will if I have time. I might have to drive my husband to work. He may start work at 8:00, or he may start work at 12:00. His schedule changes a lot.

Lien: Thanks anyway. I'll ask my father. Maybe he'll be able to drive me.

Your Turn

With a partner, talk about the different ways you are able to travel. For example, say "I can't take the train because I work nights, and there are no trains early in the morning. I might be able to take the bus. There's a bus stop near my house."

Organizing Your Ideas

Lien can choose from many kinds of transportation in her city. Think about the ways people travel in your city. List the types of transportation on the left in the chart below. Then, on the right, list the advantages and disadvantages of each.

Types of Transportation	Advantages	Disadvantages
walk	cheap good exercise	takes a lot of time

What kind(s) of transportation do you think people in your city will use in the future? Do you think you will buy a car some day? How about an electric car? Will people travel around the city by train? (Maybe your city doesn't have a train system today, but maybe it will have trains in the future.)

Future Types of Travel	Advantages	Disadvantages

Talk About It

In a group, talk about the kinds of transportation in your city today and possible kinds of transportation in the future. How do you come to school? How long does it take you to come to school? How will you be able to travel around the city in the future?

Issues and Answers

Lien's friend, Juan, has a problem. Read the letter and Anita's advice. Then talk with other students about the advice. Do you agree? What other advice can you give?

Ask Abdul and Anita

DEAR ANITA,

I have a problem with my neighbor. He often asks me to drive him to work or other places. I'm happy to help him, but the extra gas and other costs are expensive, and he never gives me any money for the rides. I want to be friendly and helpful to my neighbor, but I'm also trying to save $100 a month to buy myself a different used car in the future. I'm not able to save much money because all the rides I give him cost me a lot of money. What should I do?

—JUAN

DEAR JUAN,

It's not fair of your neighbor to ask you for rides and not give you money for expenses. You ought to figure out a fair price for the rides and then ask your neighbor to help you with your car expenses. He can pay per mile or per trip. Then you will be able to save some money to buy a car in the future. You should also help your friend learn how to use public transportation. Then he might not need rides from you! Good luck!

—ANITA

Your Turn

Juan needs to make a list of the expenses he has for his car, to help him decide how much money his neighbor should give him for the rides.

Step 1: With a partner, make a list of the expenses Juan has for his car. How much money should Juan ask his neighbor to pay? Do you think Juan should charge for every mile or for every trip?

Step 2: Look at the charts on page 118. What transportation in your city can Juan help his friend use? Should Juan's friend use public transportation or ask Juan for rides and pay him for his expenses?

Step 3: Share the list you made in Step 1 with the class. Then tell the class about the decisions you made in Step 2.

Community Involvement

It's important to learn about the different types of transportation in your community. It's a good idea to make a list of telephone numbers and other important information about transportation in your city. You might also want to get bus schedules and train schedules for your area of town.

Your Turn

With a partner, talk about traveling in a city in the United States and in your native country. Was it easy to get around in your native country? Was it easy and convenient to get around the city when you first came to the United States? Do you have any problems now? Which city has better public transportation: the city where you lived in your native country, or the city you live in today?

Community Action

Step 1: With a partner, find information about different types of transportation in your community. Look in a telephone book, newspaper, or go on the Internet. Find the answers to these questions.

- What is the name of the bus company? What is its phone number?
- Is there a train or subway? What is its phone number?
- What is the name of a taxi company and its phone number?
- How much does the taxi company charge per mile?

Step 2: Make a chart like the one below in your notebook. Write the information you found in your chart.

Method of Transportation	Phone number	Starting location near my house or school	Cost/other information
City Train Transit	1-800-723-4352	Train stop at Elm and 43rd St.	$1.50 and up $11 to airport
Taxi		Door to door	

Talk About It

In a group talk about the transportation information you wrote on your chart. What public transportation is near your school? What is the cheapest way for you to get around the city? What is the fastest way for you to travel in your city?

💡 Wrap Up

Lien looked at train and bus schedules to find the best way to get around Los Angeles. What is the best way to get around in your city? Work in a group and imagine that you are helping someone new in your city. Choose the three best kinds of transportation in your city. Write the kind of transportation, costs, advantages, and disadvantages in the chart below.

	#1	#2	#3
Kinds of transportation			
Costs			
Advantages			
Disadvantages			

With a partner, talk about transportation in your city. Use words from the unit, **should, ought to, can, able to, may,** and **might.** For example:

A: I need to go to a job interview in the city. What's the best way to get there?
B: Oh, you should take the bus.
A: I don't think I'll be able to take the bus. There isn't a stop near my house.
B: Can you take the train? It's more expensive, but it's faster than the bus.
A: I might be able to take the train. I'll have to check the schedule.

Practice your conversation. Then share it with the class.

Think About Learning

Check (✓) to show your learning in this unit. Then write one more thing you learned.

SKILLS / STRUCTURES	PAGE	EASY 😊	SO-SO 😐	DIFFICULT 😟
Talk about rules, advantages and disadvantages of of public transportation	110, 114			
Understand conversations about public transportation	111, 115			
Give advice with **should** and **ought to**	112			
Read a train schedule	113			
Use **can** and **be able to**	117			
Use **may** and **might**	116			
Learn about transportation in your community	118, 120			
Plan the best way to get around your city	118, 121			
Compare public and private transportation	119			

Common Comparative and Superlative Adjectives

Comparative Adjectives

For one-syllable adjectives, add **-er.** Add only an **-r** to one-syllable adjectives ending in **-e** or **-ee.**

> fast—faster   cheap—cheaper   large—larger

For one-syllable adjectives ending in a single vowel and a single consonant, double the consonant and add **-er.**

> big—bigger   thin—thinner   hot—hotter

If the adjective ends in **-w** or **-x**, add **-er.**

> slow—slower   narrow—narrower

If a one-or two-syllable adjective ends in **-y**, change the **-y** to **-i** and add **-er.**

> shy—shier   easy—easier   heavy—heavier

For other adjectives with two or more syllables, use **more.**

> expensive—more expensive   interesting—more interesting
> powerful—more powerful

Superlative Adjectives

For one-syllable adjectives, add **-est.** Add only an **-st** to one-syllable adjectives ending in **-e** or **-ee.**

> fast—fastest   cheap—cheapest   large—largest

For one-syllable adjectives ending in a single vowel and a single consonant, double the consonant and add **-est.**

> big—biggest   thin—thinnest   hot—hottest

If the adjective ends in **-w** or **-x**, add **-est.**

> slow—slowest   narrow—narrowest

If a one-or two-syllable adjective ends in **-y**, change the **-y** to **-i** and add **-est.**

> shy—shiest   easy—easiest   heavy—heaviest

For other adjectives with two or more syllables, use **most.**

> expensive—most expensive   interesting—most interesting
> powerful—most powerful

Irregular Adjectives

Base Form	Comparative	Superlative
good, well	better	best
bad	worse	worst
far	farther	farthest
fun	more fun	most fun